THE
COTSWOLDS
LIFE AND TRADITIONS

THE
COTSWOLDS
LIFE AND TRADITIONS

JUNE LEWIS

WEIDENFELD & NICOLSON

LONDON

For Ralph

for all the best reasons

© George Weidenfeld and Nicolson Limited 1996

Text © June Lewis 1996

First published in 1996 by
George Weidenfeld and Nicolson Limited
The Orion Publishing Group
Orion House
5 Upper St Martin's Lane
London WC2H 9EA

British Library
Cataloguing in Publication Data
A catalogue record for this book is avaliable from the British Library.

Edited, designed and typeset by Playne Books
Trefin Pembrokeshire

Editor Gill Davies
Designer David Playne

Printed and bound in Italy

Front cover photograph
The May fair at Letchlade

Back cover photograph
Netting for pike, 1911

Photograph opposite title page
William Ash and his daughter.
William is wearing 'knee belts' to
prevent mice running up his trouser legs.

Contents page left hand side photograph
The tricycling tramp of Macaroni Woods

Contents page right hand side photograph
Dr Powell with an eighteen-pound pike,
which in turn contained a moorhen.

Contents

Foreword by Pam Ayres

I fell in love with the Cotswolds when I worked in a dull engineering works outside Witney. At lunchtime I used to rush out for air and if I looked sharp about it, I could walk down to the nearby village of Crawley and spend a few minutes walking along the Windrush river. It was a very soothing river to follow, with bent-over willow trees, creamy drystone walls, and old soft-coloured buildings which so belonged to the scene that they might have just grown up out of the ground one fertile spring. One day, in a ditch adjoining the river I saw the exposed backs of two pike, tough predators innocently sunning themselves in the shallow water. It was all a great antidote to the oily world of engineering. On other days I would drop down through the wood piquantly known as Maggots Grove to stand and stare at the towering ruins of Minster Lovell Hall. In time I followed the river beyond Burford and gradually, little piece by little piece, I came to know more of the true Cotswolds and to love their gentle colours and unique scale. I missed it when I went away and looked forward to seeing it again, as if it were some kind and comfortable old friend.

The joy of June Lewis's wonderful book, *The Cotswolds: Life and Traditions*, is that it takes us beneath this familiar surface, beyond what we can actually see and affectionately, layer by layer, uncovers the events and influences which shaped the countryside and people of the Cotswolds. June has the ability to bring history vividly to life, and to make it relevant today. Illustrated by a most poignant collection of photographs, and by a wealth of diary fragments, recipes and household accounts, she builds up a fascinating and comprehensive picture of what life was really like. Her book is filled with information but at the same time sprinkled with wonderfully touching and humorous moments. I recommend the recipe for one hundred gallons of Workhouse soup which calls for sixty-three pounds of clods and stickings!

It has been my own good fortune to escape from that engineering factory, to find interesting work and international travel and I have found one thing to be true. However brief a glimpse they may have had, people do not forget the Cotswolds. I have seen the name kindle a smile on the grimmest face in the most remote of places.

June Lewis has lived in the Cotswolds all her life, and so has her family for as far back as records can be traced. In this, her eighth book about the area, she shares her great knowledge and unquenchable enthusiasm. I hope this richly informative book helps everyone who reads it to derive more pleasure and interest from a visit to the Cotswolds and to better appreciate the character and beauty of the area by knowing something of what made it as it is today.

I asked June about her amazing knowledge of the Cotswolds area. She said 'I love it. There's always some-thing new to learn and I just can't get enough of it.'

I hope her book makes you feel the same.

Pam Ayres

Introduction

Admirers of the Cotswold landscape are well served by the quantity of literature available. Millions of words have been written in admiration of the region's scenery and sense of uniformity in its architecture. Not all this quantity of output is matched by quality, however, and the resident or visitor to the district, or student from afar, must exercise judgement in assessing its value.

It is also perhaps harder in the Cotswolds than in some other well-preserved rural areas to gain a depth of feeling for the way of life of the community in past times, as opposed to the physical remains of buildings, houses and antiquities which we preserve according to the fashion of the late twentieth century.

What was life like for the villager in Ebrington or Ampney Crucis before the first world war? What factors shaped the life of the village communities throughout the district and how are they recorded? Who were the great families of the area?

Such questions are the very stuff of local historical research and attract an increasing number of enquirers every year to public libraries and museums. Local history is a growth area, as people take the time to look around them at what has gone before and seek to know more.

Often such studies begin with a particular theme or episode from the historical record. The story of the seventeenth century Civil War and its effect upon the communities across the Cotswolds is well recorded (and endlessly fascinating) and thus a relatively easy subject to pursue. But — in another century — who was Betty of Betty's Grave, near Poulton just outside Cirencester? Where and when does she fit into the local story and who can tell us the story anyway?

Here, in a world where local history evidence interlinks both the soundly documented to the purely anecdotal, June Lewis has made a significant contribution to Cotswold studies. *The Cotswolds: Life and Traditions* joins an impressive array of her published studies, both books and articles, all with a recurring theme of Cotswold local history. The fruits of many years of research both in conversation as well as in the library and record office come together in the easy flow of this compilation.

Where else would we find together the story of Benedictus Grace, rogue vicar of Ampney in the seventeenth century, and — in another century but in many ways not so far removed — a delightful vignette of splendidly-named Fly-o-Gert, hawker and manipulator of female minds wrestling with the task of making inadequate ends meet? There is a direct link between these two accounts, one now only available to us because it was written down ('documented' in the way of curators and archivists), the other because it is an oral record, passed down by recollection and written into studies of this kind. The recording process goes hand in hand with authorship and carries a responsibility for accuracy. Newspaper reports of earlier centuries should be read with the same caution with which we might approach the press today.

None the less, with this proviso, the local press has continued to preserve a vast and colourful archive of historical information. Thus we are able to read how the 'momentous news' of the ending of the Boer War had to take its place in Fairford alongside great excitement for the locals because the 'May-fly was up' on the river Coln's renowned fishing waters.

June Lewis makes excellent use of the contemporary record in her description of Cotswold life and traditions. The official records of school, workhouse and public authority stand here alongside the diaries of individuals, the press reports of events and activities, and the whole array of local paper 'ephemera' (so collectable nowadays) which give the Cotswold story its human face.

Here we can find village children recorded absent from school in 1908 because they were picking dandelions to make wine, and (a personal favourite) the closure of Guiting Power village school for the afternoon on 8 January 1934 'as the Point-to-Point Races were again at Roel Gate and the majority of parents attend with their children'.

No studies of Cotswold history can be complete without an assessment of the significance of the wool trade in the life and wealth of the district, and the contribution which the winning and use of Cotswold stone has made to the man-made face of the environment. June Lewis plays to her strengths here, using her considerable knowledge to good effect.

The flow of Cotswold books, both specialist and general, shows no sign of slackening, and it could be argued that better access to the vast array of documents in record offices and libraries — as well as artefacts in museums — is stimulating an improved quality of study. This volume deserves to take its place alongside an earlier and well-respected examination of Cotswold life and tradition by Edith Brill in 1973, and to enjoy equal success.

Those whose life and traditions such volumes record, such as George Swinford of Filkins or James Rathbone, champion blacksmith, may pass on, but their contribution to the communities in which they lived and worked will not now be forgotten — thanks to studies of the kind which June Lewis has made.

We need not ask whether such 'characters' still exist, as we live in a world entirely differently structured from the one they knew. We do, however, continue to make our own local — as well as national — history and should always be alert to the need to keep the best possible record of our own lifestyles, so that future historians can document us in our turn.

Fly-o-Gert may have gone but her philosophy of selling can still be found hidden within the apparently more sophistoicated ways of the present generation.

David Viner
Curator of Museums
Corinium Museum, Cirencester
Cotswold Countryside Collection, Northleach
February 1996

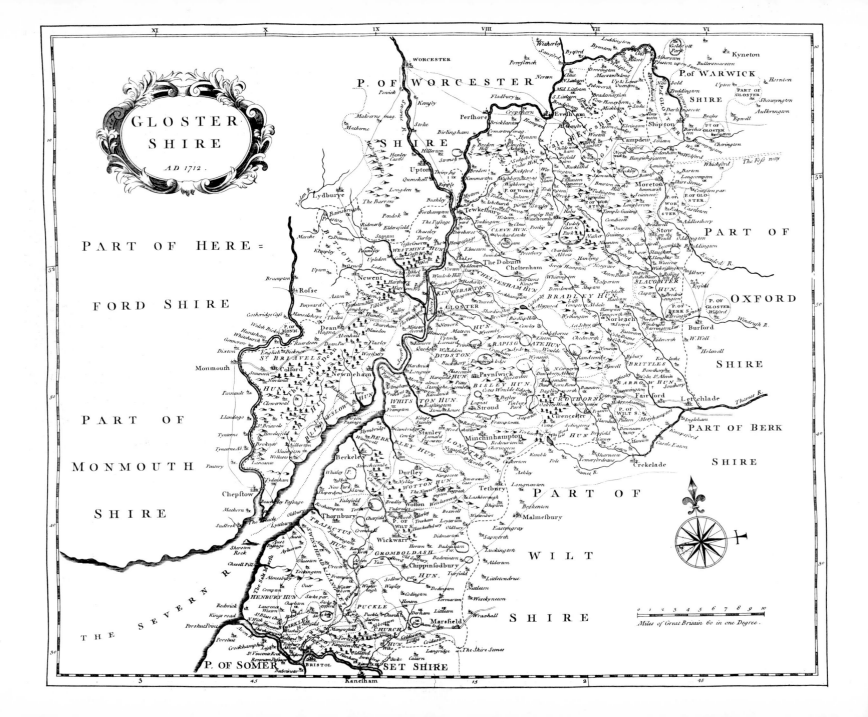

THE COTSWOLD HILLS

There was such beauty in the dappled valley
As hurt the sight, as stabbed the heart to tears.
The gathered loveliness of all the years
Hovered thereover, it seemed, eternally

Ivor Gurney

Poets, authors and artists have been inspired to capture the spirit of the Cotswolds throughout the centuries; it is a spirit which can sometimes seem elusive in definition but, as Ivor Gurney so eloquently put it, 'the gathered loveliness' seems to hover eternally. It is a consistent, rather than an ephemeral, quality of the Cotswolds scene.

Geographically, the Cotswolds are an area in the heartland of England; a wedge of hill country running from Chipping Campden in the north to Bath at the southernmost tip, tapering from the western edge of the escarpment across to the Windrush Valley on the eastern side and narrowed to half its breadth by the Upper Thames watershed cutting its own boundary from Lechlade to Oxfordshire.

Topographically, it is the six-hundred square miles of the belt of oolitic limestone which is the widest part as it runs from Dorset to Yorkshire, and lies mainly in Gloucestershire. The relief of the Cotswolds is the dramatic scarpline which emerged ten thousand years ago as the last of the Ice Age released its grip on the land. The land itself was formed some 180 million years before that, and that embryonic stage has left its imprint in the stone in the form of minutae of shells and subterranean deposits which give such character to the texture and tone of the buildings and miles of dry stone walls. Viewed from the vale to the west, the escarpment runs as an unbroken frontier boundary, undulating gently from the south, deeply wooded valleys curling the edges from Wotton under its own little promontory, defining the Stroud pitches and bottoms, to arc above Gloucester and Cheltenham before reaching its highest peak at Cleeve Cloud where it reaches just over a thousand feet. The Common plateau is the wildest area in the region and leads to the high wold country of the North Cotswolds, with combes cutting dips and dells into the rolling hillside as it climbs to Chipping Campden, to level into Shakespeare's Avon vale.

Historically, it is the scarp edge which holds the chronological catalogue of life on the Cotswolds, for it is punctuated with the remains of neolithic hill-forts — grass-covered humps and hollows on the landscape provide visible evidence of a long past settlement, such as excavated at Crickley Hill. These were defence points from which tribal chieftains could keep watch on any advances made by invading forces. From the extent of their enclosures it would indicate such hill-forts became crudely constructed commercial centres for the marketing of cattle. The long barrows of the New Stone Age people give us the earliest example of how the stone on the Cotswolds was used as a construction material. Still on the escarpment line, at Belas Knap, the skill of dry stone walling, as practised by men who lived three thousand years before the Saxon invasion, is an enduring monument to the communion of man with nature. The ragstone, of little more than an inch in thickness, demonstrates the art of building a dry stone wall which has become the outstanding feature of Cotswold country; the placing of the stones one over two and two over one providing such a close adhesion by their compounded weight that it would be impossible to run a knife blade between them, making mortar totally unnecessary. Hetty Pegler's Tump, near Stroud, affords closer examination as the narrow stone-roofed chamber can be visited. It is the resting place of a people who had started farming.

The Romans imprinted their occupation of the Cotswolds by marching out their ruler-straight roads and from their civilization sprang the improvement of the native stock of sheep. By the time the farming Saxons settled on the wolds around the seventh century, the large-framed sheep had evolved into heavy fleece-bearing animals thriving on the rich herbage of the limestone country.

Culturally, Cotswold life and tradition stem from the Anglo-Saxon period. The majority of place-names in the region have their roots in that age; the land and life on the land were the pivotal point from which ritual and custom sprang to form a seasonal cycle, their pagan origins embraced into the Church calendar as the Church became the most powerful land-owner before the Norman Invasion. The distinctive dialect was born out of the way of life led in this hilly wold country and although the custom and culture are not tangible in the way that the Cotswold vernacular applies to the outstanding architecture, they give an almost equally palpable quality and identity to the region.

The Cotswolds are distinctive. Their gentle dipping, eastward from the uptilted escarpment, gives the rise and fall of wold and wooded valley dotted with old market towns and secluded villages, raised from the stone beneath the very feet of the builders in a style suited to the social time and scale, to withstand the prevailing weather conditions and not the capricious master of fashion. Equally distinctive are the folk who live and work here; they are quintessentially English. Collectively they are instantly identifiable, but it is a unity devoid of uniformity, for within the homogenous whole is the individual, the essential eccentricities which give cadence and colour to a culture.

To many, the Cotswolds will appear a microcosm of Britain's past. The landscape which did not lend itself to large-scale manufacturing and rail and water transport routes imposed its own limitations on industrial advances. Refractory landowners could not be blasted out of their entrenched autonomy with gunpowder and pickaxe. It took two world wars to finally shake the old social order from its feudal roots, yet there is much unchanged, unspoilt in the general ethos of what has been officially recognized as an area of outstanding natural beauty but one which has not stagnated into a museum piece.

In the Cotswolds, life and traditions have sprung from the hills and valleys and have survived there, the

Nailsworth
from Watledge Hill 1854

landscape providing a natural frontier to the worst aspects of industrialization. Many valleys were still accessible only by donkey when the Arts and Crafts movement sought out these surroundings and their choice was not an arbitrary one. Against this background of tenacity to tradition and ties to the land, age-old crafts have continued to serve the immediate community and the close integration of lives and landscape is still apparent. This communion and continuity, together with a unique blend of stone buildings with hill and vale, is the legacy that encapsulates 'the gathered loveliness of all the years'.

LIFE
IN THE
COMMUNITY

Edward Wheeler, Hasleton postman, setting off to deliver letters to Salperton and Compton Abdale. He later used a pony and trap.

Church
and Chapel

'As sure as God's in Gloucestershire'

The humble little parish church at Hailes survived its aristocratic abbey neighbour and has served the community for some eight hundred and fifty years.

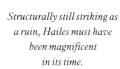

Structurally still striking as a ruin, Hailes must have been magnificent in its time.

This old saying, taken as a kind of oath in everyday speech much as we say nowadays 'as true as I stand here', is believed to have stemmed from the extraordinary number of holy places built in the county. The Cotswolds have a rich heritage of ancient churches and chapelries tucked into the folds of the wolds.

Another school of thought is that the saying originated from the belief that the Holy Blood was at Hailes Abbey — fostered by Chaucer who refers in the Pardoner's Tale to 'the blode of Crist that is in Hayles'. Such was the fame of the abbey, founded in 1246 by Richard, Earl of Cornwall (the younger brother of Henry III), as a thanksgiving for surviving a shipwreck, that the Cistercian abbey was the magnet for pilgrims from far and wide, including the temperamental Tudor, Henry VIII. Wreaking vengeful anger against the abbey when his scientists analysed the sacred relic, authenticated by Pope Urban IV, as nothing holier than duck's blood, the grandeur and power that Hailes had enjoyed over three centuries were reduced to naught as it was sacked and pillaged.

Prinknash —commanding Elyseum

'It stands on a glorious but
impracticable hill,
in the midst of a little forest of beech,
and commanding Elyseum'

Horace Walpole 1744

*The monks laying the base
of the roadway to
Prinknash abbey in 1939.
The outline of the new
abbey foundations can be
seen in the background.*

The grange and hunting lodge of the thirteenth-century abbots of Gloucester became the fine Tudor manor to which Henry VIII came with his vivacious Ann Boleyn. Later the monks of the Benedictine order settled the first monastic order in the Cotswolds since the Dissolution when they built the new abbey in 1928. In the spirit of their order, the Benedictine monks of Prinknash set about building their own abbey when they outgrew the old grange. Four months after its foundation stone was laid in 1939 the Second World War broke out. During ensuing years building came to a virtual halt and it was another thirty-three years to the day from when the foundation stone was laid before the new building was consecrated.

Rich and glowing, some 2,500 tons of the deeply hued ashlar, the golden stone from Guiting, was dressed by the monks themselves. As the first boatload of monks left their former home at Caldey they passed under a rainbow over the Sound. Although they did not find gold upon arrival, when the foundations were being dug for the new abbey they came across a seam of clay. Brothers Thomas and Basil experimented with it on a wheel in a garden shed. From their first couple of pots, thrown to help out with the abbey's house keeping, evolved the distinctive and world-famed Prinknash pottery. Prinknash, keeping faith with its monastic traditions, is almost totally self-supporting.

Viewed from the gateway of the herb-filled monastery garden, the sun of three hundred summers warming its Regency walls, is the old grey-stoned grange still serving the Benedictine community, overlooking not only Elyseum but the vibrant pulse of continuity into the twentieth century. And rooted even further back into its tradition is the tramps' shelter, outside the kitchen door, where truly penniless and needy travellers can still receive refreshment.

Priory to Parish Church to Barn

At Leonard Stanley there is an ancient church
Where Roman Catholics were wont to search
  For miracles and relics that will give
  To any sinful wretch a quick reprieve
The artful monks to cheat the humble poor
  Were hid in winding passages secure
  To mimic supernatural voices when
They wanted to defraud their fellowmen
The priory adjoining where the nuns toll'd o'er
  Their beads, and veiled their faces once
Is now a farmer's dwelling, richly stored
With all that's needful for the festive board
The place where devotees and friars trod
Bearing the Host which they revered as God
Is now a haunt for poultry, geese and swine
Where people feed and milk their useful kine

The barn referred to at Leonard Stanley dates back to the Saxon farming era and originated as the priory church (founded by Roger de Berkeley) which suffered destruction in the dissolution of the monasteries. With fortunate foresight as it turned out, the parishioners' church was built to the west of the monastic campus and escaped the fate of its near neighbour but not, according to the rhyming tale above, the monkish pranks of the early inhabitants. Villagers have, into quite recent times, reported the presence of a phantom figure in the church.

Cotswold wool churches

There are four outstanding examples of medieval churches that the wealthy wool merchants built, or re-built, on the site of an earlier church. These are all Perpendicular in style, of the finest stonework, lofty and spacious, and attractively grouped in their old market towns.

Chipping Campden, Fairford, and Northleach all have brasses depicting the merchants in the dress of the day. Lechlade owes its church of St Lawrence to the pious munifence of the wool merchants. Like Northleach in the mid-Cotswolds, the church corners the marketplace.

The smallest and largest

Beyond the willow-fringed meadows of the Dikler is the smallest church in the Cotswolds at Clapton-on-the-Hill, a chapelry of Bourton-on-the-Water. The little church offers a promise of 'indulgence for the devout' within its old stone walls, and an ingenious design of horseshoes acts as the churchyard gate.

The church of St John the Baptist dominates the centre of Cirencester, itself the capital of the Cotswolds; the largest parish church in the county — larger, it is claimed, than three of England's cathedrals. The fine Perpendicular tower rises some 134 feet. As Corinium under the Roman occupation, Cirencester was the second largest city in the country and the church stands right over the line of the famous Roman road, Ermine Street. Saxon and Norman, in their turn, founded churches on the site and traces of their hand can be seen in the present church.

Its peal of twelve bells adds distinction befitting its grandeur. The original eight were saved by the townspeople in 1634 when, down for re-casting, the Parliamentarians had their eye on them for cannon metal. The sum of thirty pounds was raised to 'buy' them back for the church. A bell from the ancient St John's Hospital was given to the church some two decades later. This ninth bell is known locally as the Pancake Bell, as it was rung on Shrove Tuesday: 'Pan On, Pan On', it called and, according to a long cherished legend, that stirred not only the housewives to use up their flour and eggs before Lent fasting, but was a signal for the parish pump to make its annual

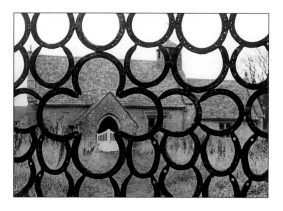

*The church at
Clapton-on-the-Hill
— seen through the horse
shoe gate.*

*St John the Baptist,
Cirencester.*

walk round the Market Place! The tenth bell of the peal was the curfew bell, tolling at eight o'clock during the winter evenings — a custom dating back to Norman times.

Bell with no Church

The Cotswolds abound with mysteries and folklore. One such story concerns the bell at Frocester. Only the medieval bell tower remains of the old village which was destroyed by fire and rebuilt about a mile away. The tale goes that the bell-ringers of Coaley planned to steal the bell from the abandoned Frocester tower and, under cover of darkness, manoeuvred it halfway down the stairs. Having left it there, to rest from their labours a while, they returned to find an old lady sitting on top of it. Despite coaxing and cajoling her to move, she heeded them not. When one of the ringers grew angry and tried to push her off, she vanished into thin air — and the terrified ringers rushed home. It was thought that the guardian of the bell was probably the spirit of the lady who had thrown her jewels into the metal as it was being cast. The bell had been her gift to the church.

Quenington's unique treasure

The Romanesque doorways of St Swithins Church at Quenington in the Coln Valley are unique to a village church. Of incredibly fine and imaginative detail, the north door tympanum depicts the Harrowing of Hell, while the south tympanum portraying the Coronation of the Virgin is the first known in Europe, after Reading Abbey, which depicts the Coronation in this way. It is probable that the Norman doorways were made for the church in the late twelfth century when Agnes and her daughter Sibyl de Lacy founded the preceptory of Knights Hospitallers of St John of Jerusalem in the village. It is known that the Hospitallers

Detail of the Coronation of the Virgin tympanum.

Percy Bysshe Shelley and the old path named after him, 'Shelley's Walk'.

obtained the church, after a wrangle, and held land at Quenington and in the surrounding parishes until the Dissolution.

Sweet secrets

Here could I hope that death did hide from human
sight sweet secrets
Percy Bysshe Shelley 1815

Percy Bysshe Shelley, one of England's greatest lyric poets, was inspired by the church of St Lawrence to compose *Stanzas in Lechlade Churchyard* on a summer evening during the peak of his poetical genius at the age of twenty-seven. The walk linking the Market Place to the old wharf lane leading to the Thames has now been named after the poet.

Bidfield, Bisley and Bibury

High up on the hills between Birdlip and Stroud once stood Bidfield, an isolated outpost of the ecclesiastical parish of Bisley. Today only a farmhouse and cottages remain of what was once was a complete community — but excavations for a new road have revealed the site of the town church and manor house. Just when the medieval settlement was abandoned is not altogether clear, but old tales cannot be buried like buildings and echoes of long ago linger in folk memory and have been passed down through the centuries in true oral inheritance.

The good folk of Bidfield, it is said, had a church built outside the parish boundary of Bisley to appease both God and king. This action became necessary when the king forbade them to worship in their own church. The church's silver bells were supposedly buried in the churchyard.

Bisley survived where Bidfield perished, but it is a legend-locked place. When the church was being built it was thought that Old Nick himself kept moving the stones about during the night so that the masons were all of a flummox finding them, and the cause of their moving, the next morning.

Then, when the church was finally raised, the village was ex-communicated by the Pope because a priest fell down the well one dark night. To avoid a recurrence, the well was built over and an intricately carved stone Poor Soul's Light erected, containing candles for masses to be said for the poor.

Meanwhile, the penalty for losing the priest in such a careless way was a two-year ban on burying their dead in their own churchyard. They were obliged to carry their departed some fifteen miles to Bibury to be interred in the churchyard there. A section in Bibury churchyard is called 'the Bisley Piece', and several old maps show the route between the two villages marked as Dead Man's Lane.

Poor Souls' Light at Bisley.

Ashbrook Police Station diary 1846: it was an offence to open public or beer houses during the hours of 'Divine Service'.

Rent, rates and regulations

The church was once the very hub of the community's life. It was here that the first schooling was taught, music made, plays performed and fairs held in the churchyard. Church bells rang in celebration and in warning; the curfew bell was rung in some places in the Cotswolds until the outbreak of war, when the ringing of church bells ceased —except for invasion. The church was also the place where the parish fire engine was kept, and in most places it was the tolling of the fifth bell of the peal that called the brigade together to manhandle the cart and buckets.

It is remembered how on one occasion — when they were called to a rick fire in the north Cotswolds — by the time one team had loaded the beer barrel on to the cart and caught and harnessed up the horse, the farmer had subdued the flames a bit. The captain, falling over the hose in the pitch dark night, shouted to the farmer, 'Get that fire going again, will ye, so as we can see what we be about'.

In the past the church had more power than the state, and some old laws lingered on well into Victorian times. Regulations on opening times of public houses were tied to those of divine service in each parish. An entry from Ashbrook Police diary of 1846 shows the village bobby had to patrol the area during church service times to ensure adherence to the law.

Rates of the ancient system of recompensing God under the law of deodands, abolished in 1846, fluctuated considerably. An extract from a coroner's journal of 1805:

July 3rd, 1805

To attending Adam Perrott's at Nibley on the body of Nath Higgs, late of Yate, mason: killed whilst at work in a well belonging to ye said Perrott at Nibley, by a large stone, supposed six hundredweight, falling from out of the side of the well upon his body, which caused instant death.

In this case the deodand was assessed at the derisory sum of one penny, the entry showing that the Lord of the Manor was responsible for payment.

Rent for pews constituted a seating hierarchy in the congregation. When one lady who had refused to pay a pew rent was spotted by the eagle-eyed clerk enjoying someone else's 'paid pew' and was politely reminded that she was in the wrong seat, she replied, 'I sat in this seat for The Creation, and I intend to remain here for The Last Judgment!'

Robert Raikes in 1794 wrote of his Sunday School treat where 'a plentiful dinner' was served up: 'I wish you could step in and see what clean and joyous countenances we shall exhibit, a scene for an epicure in philanthropy.'

Rural rides in farm wagons to a hayfield some mile or two away, with baskets of bread and cheese, cake and stone casks of ale, were the delights to which church and chapel goers looked forward until the advent of the railways brought trips to the seaside on excursion trains to widen their horizons.

Religious persecution

During the ravages of the Civil War, Burford's lovely old church was a prison for some three hundred and forty Levellers. One left his identity roughly chiselled in the font: 'Anthony Sedley, 1649. Prisner'. A century earlier Burford was the scene of bigoted religious persecution in 1521 when the penalty for crimes ranged from public display to painful dispatch.

'Everyone to go upon a market day thrice about the market of Burford, and then to stand up upon the highest steps of the cross there, a quarter of an hour, with a faggot of wood upon his shoulder ... also to beare a faggot of wood before the procession on a certain Sunday at Burford from the Quire doore going out, to the quire doore going in, and once to bear a faggot at the burning of a heretic ... also none of

Chapel teas and Sunday school treats were highlights of the Victorian calendar: tea meeting at Winston.

them to hide their [branded in cross] mark upon their cheek ... in the event of refusal, they were to be given up to the civil authorities to be burnt.'

Heresy was very much a matter of hearsay. A not-so-loyal servant of the Reverend John Drury at Windrush had his master indicted for bemoaning the waste of his eighteen pence on pilgrimage to Hailes and for declaring the holy relic 'a fabrication of men's hands'. Villagers vilified their vicars in the upheavals of the Civil War and another incumbent of Windrush was made to carry a bundle of faggots thrice round the cross at Burford for keeping a concubine.

If the political leanings of the parson opposed those of his congregation he was in for a rough time. Records tell of priests being pushed into the open graves of those they were burying, 'bibs and gowns cut off' and services disrupted by raucous heckling.

Parsons: good sports and other sorts

Two Victorian parsons, renowned for hunting the fox instead of stray souls, were the Reverend Joseph Pitt of Rendcomb and the Reverend Henry Prowse Jones of Edgeworth. Joe Pitt is said to have entertained the Prince of Wales while hunting with the Cotswold Hunt, and often visited his parishioners in his boots and breeches. The Reverend Henry Jones is credited with sending the following lines to one of his young lady parishioners who had voiced her misgivings as to whether parsons should hunt.

To Diana, not of the Ephesians

On Sunday next, I'll take my text,
From Holy writs' record,
Wherein we're told, how Nimrod bold,
Hunted before the Lord.

And whilst I preach, I'll strive to teach
That hunting on a Monday
Will not efface, nor yet disgrace,
My doctrine on a Sunday.

And should the Bishop, dare to dish up,
His ire on any grounds,
I'll prove the fact, by an old Act,
He's bound to keep some hounds.

Whilst lovely Miss, you ponder this,
To vow you'll soon begin;
Parsons may hunt, as they are wont,
Without committing sin.

The Reverend William Cockin, also a hunting parson, is said to have obtained the living of Minchinhampton by the toss of a coin while a dinner guest at Gatcombe House, the home of David Ricardo. The last rector of the original parish, Ricardo built Amberley church as a thanksgiving for his son's miraculous escape from a riding accident in Gatcombe Park. It took eleven days to sell the contents of his wine cellar when he died in 1841!

In his notebooks Kingscote Daunt records:

June 14th 1750

An account of my Personal Estate, Goods and Chattels Mr Warneford owes me £10. *

A study of books value	£40 0s 0d
A Burow (presumably —bureau)	£3 3s 0d
A Tea Chest	7s 6d
A table cloth, napkins and towells	£1 1s 0d
A tobacco dish	2s 6d
A silver Watch made by Tompion	£5 5s 0d
The Pictures of the Royal Family	£1 1s 0d
The Pictures in my Study and Elsewhere	£1 1s 0d
Brought home (from Bath) two Moidores and silver	£3 0s 0d
4 Johns	£14 8s 0d
One John	£3 12s 0d
Remainder 2 saddles	
My wearing apparel of every kind	
My Canonical Habits	£6 7s 0d
Total	£24 7s 0d

* Mr Warneford was the Rector, who seemed to be in the habit of paying his curate very late.

I commenced Curate of Owlpen, December 14, 1748, according to Mr Warneford's own Letter.
I received £38 17s on December 24, 1748

lent my father out of Midsummer half-rent 1748	£9 9s 0d
lent my father again	£8 13s 0d
my father paid £2 7s	
paid Thomas Pierce for Shooing	2s 6d
gave the Maid at Christmas	1s 0d
gave Tyndal the Fiddler at twice	2s 0d
laid out with the Scotchman	£1 8s 6d
gave Doctor Perry for advice	10s 6d
paid out of my Christmas Rent, 1748 to William	11s 0d
paid for exchanging bill	3s 10d
to Clarke and spent at Dursley	4s 3d
paid my Brother	£2 4s 0d
paid my Mother	14s 0d
paid Mr Colborne the Apothecary	£2 7s 0d
paid for Mr Ledwel's cheese	£1 6s 0d
laid out with the Pedlar	£1 11s 6d
gave the Physician	10s 6d
paid for several things	5s 6d
paid for Oats to my Brother	8s 0d
paid for Two pair of Shoos	10s 0d
paid a Quarter's Shaving	4s 6d
paid Roger Lord the Taylor	£1 18s 0d
paid John Fereby for making my breeches	7s 6d
paid for making three Shirts	6s 0d
paid Mr Scott for a brown wigg	£1 1s 0d
paid for a qr of Tobacco	6d
paid for a Saddle Cloth, &c	£2 10s 0d
paid Mr Huntridge the Surgeon	£1 1s 0d
paid Gabriel Barns for Wine	£1 1s 0d
spent at Tetbury twice and at Wotton	10s 0d
paid Mr Vines for Rum	10s 0d
paid to Mr Wightwick for Potter the Barber	£1 1s 0d
I have money remaining — one three pound twelve	£3 12s 0d
10 pieces at 1:16:0 each	£18 0s 0d
4 Guineas	£4 4s 0d
Total	£25 16s 0d

April 27th, 1749

I received for marrying a couple 5s 0d

Begun with the Barber on Saturday, January 27th, 1749, to shave twice a week

Begun with the Gloster Journal, December 11th, 1749

Expenses at first going to Bath, 1749

paid for mending my Watch		4s 0d
a pair of Black Buckles		1s 0d
thrice going in the Cold Bath		3s 0d
a Magazine		6d
ribbands to somebody		2s 6d
horse 10 nights and Corn		7s 6d
paid the barber		2s 0d
gave the Servants at Saracens Head		3s 6d
dined twice at The Bear		4s 8d
a pair of Shoos		5s 6d
breakfast	6d	
dinner	1s	
coffea	3d	
night expences	1s 6d	
horses hay and corn per day	9d	4s 0d
Total		£1 18s 2d

The housekeeping accounts of Kingscote Daunt, Curate of Owlpen, give an interesting insight of the unbeneficed clergy in the reign of George II. The Daunt family was established at Owlpen by the time the War of the Roses pitched battle on Gloucestershire meadows when John Daunt married the heiress of the manor, Margery Owlpen.

John and Thomas Keble

The sons of the Reverend John Keble, John and Thomas, were both to make their mark in the communities they served. John influenced a radical rethink of the Anglican church, spearheading what came to be known as the Oxford Movement. Such was his impact on the academic world that he is the only person, who was neither a benefactor nor saint, to have an Oxford college named after him.

John Keble was 'a little man' when he went up to Oxford. At only fourteen years of age he won a scholarship to Corpus Christi and achieved the incredible distinction of gaining a Double First Class in Classics and Mathematics — only the second person to have done so (Robert Peel being the first), but Keble achieving it at the age of eighteen years.

John Keble senior pens fatherly advice and concern to young John at Oxford.

'...I do hereby by virtue of my parental authority lay two or three commands upon you. First take the mare at all events and resolve to sell her speedily and discretely as the best way of keeping your bones from surgeons in future and your clothes from mud. Perhaps John your porter will be a better privy counsellor upon the subject than the cunning fellow at the Corpus stables.... Your mother and I are delighted with your accounts of your progress. Your Ma just now is eating lamb and gooseberry pye with Miss Luckman while I write this admirable epistle.'

1813. 'My dear John ...I feel myself grow prouder and prouder as I grow old. Your mother with kind love sends some of the stockings, the rest are not finished. Thomas sends a letter to which I shall add a Greek exercise. I hope you get a place on the coach to return home. We think you may venture to consign your clothes and linen to the elderwine box and employ your bedmaker to cord it as firmly as possible. Before you return to college we will try to procure a good

John Keble as a young man. He was educated at home by his father, vicar at Coln St Aldwyns, until he won a scholarship to Oxford at the age of fourteen.

portmanteau. It will not be necessary to bring your surplice and sheets but give your slaves a strict charge to take care of what you leave. You will soon need a pair of boots and I recommend it to you to observe a little what is in the prevailing fashion of them in order

to give your old friend Clinch a few hints — his manufacture would certainly be preferable to that of Oxford in point of strength and cheapness. Do not on any account relax your efforts in poetry. Aunt sends a few nuts. I will send Hill with horse if you do not get coach and will send my short boots with him. Your dark trousers will accord very well with them upon the occasion. Have you paid the tradesmen's bills, and what are the sums paid to them? In what books are your lectures in now? Your mother begs you will be cautious to avoid anything likely to give you cold — damp linen and damp stockings must be guarded against.'

1806. '...So pleased Mr Darnell thinks your English verse deserving of notice. Remember what the Provost said about the subject and as to the Prize look forward to a future effort which we hope will be that your abilities will be greater than they can be expected to be at your present age.... Take care of your health, take regular exercise, enough, and not more than enough. Do not omit to take a regular walk each morning and be not tempted to pursue your studies late in the evening.'

John Keble chose to settle in the Cotswolds as a parish priest rather than become an academician. 'The first man in Oxford' was no radical; nor was he aggressive enough to be a leader, yet thinking men looked to him for guidance. Poet and scholar, he was a practical parish priest at heart and left the dreaming spires of Oxford for the pocket of parishes in the Leach and Coln Valleys, first helping his aged father, then in his own right. While at Eastleach he wrote *The Christian Year*, a collection of poems; many became favourite hymns. The stone clapper bridge linking the two parishes of Eastleach Turville with Eastleach Martin is named after this quiet cleric whose ideas rocked the foundations of the religious dogma of his day and reverberated through the whole structure of the Anglican church movement.

Thomas Keble introduced the custom of well dressing into Bisley where it still continues to mark Ascension Day.

The Seven Springs, built into the stone alcove at Bisley in 1863, were the source of drinking water for all the village.

His brother, Thomas Keble, made an impact on the village of Bisley where the effects of the Industrial Revolution brought his parishioners to stark poverty as their livelihood in the cloth industry was swept away in the changes. Full-scale charity was not in his financial power but he believed in his people keeping their self respect through employment. He drew up a scheme whereby labour was exchanged for clothing and furnishings.

A scale was drawn up relating days of work to the type of clothing: a pair of 'trowsers' was worth fifteen days' work; a common round hat, three; ladies shoes, or a pair of 'high shoes for a child', eight days; calico enough for a Sunday shirt, three days; a smock-frock suitable for working in varied from six to eight days, according to length of smock; a gingham gown with lining, six days; a straw bonnet, eight; a flannel petticoat, two. A single bedstead could be bought with labour of eighteen days; a straw mattress, six; a blanket, five and a pair of strong warm sheets, six. A Bible, prayer book, seeds and tools were assessed similarly. And, in order to keep up appearances in their adversity, the villagers 'should have his or her hair cut in decent form, a hair cutter is employed to go from house to house for this purpose'.

When plague reared its ugly head in the area in 1832, it was Keble who doled out practical advice, urging people, if they suspected they had the symptoms, to take 'castor oil with about forty drops of laudanum in it'. It was he that instituted the colourful custom of well dressing in the village; a pagan ceremony which he christianized, the great stone alcove into which seven springs have gushed water since the Iron Age is decorated with flowers by the local school children. The vicar then blesses the wells. A procession through the street and the final placing of the large frames spelling out Christian symbols and the date in fresh spring blossoms marks Ascension Day in the Cotswold village.

The ivy church of Ampney St Mary is sole survivor of the village which died around it in the Black Death.

Postlip Chapel with its Norman doorway and original Norman window was built in Stephen's reign by Sir William de Postlip, serving the hamlet community and saving them a perilous walk to the town of Winchcombe.

The vile vicar of Omenie

'To ye Honble house of Comons in the High Court of Parliamt. The humble petition of ye inhabitants of Holyrood Ampney in the County of Gloucr ...date ye 19th day of November 1640. We whose names are here subscribed humbly represent that Benedict Grace Vicar of Ampney aforesaid is a scandalous, persecuting, quarrelsome, bold, unciville and an ignorant Minister. Scandalous in yt he is given to drunkeness and lechery, persecuting in yt he commenceth very many and more unjust Suites, quarrelsome in yt he has been ye author of many frayes and Author of more assaults, bould in yt he threatens his parishioners with complynts to ye Archbishop of Canterbury, and preaching also more sermons —uncivill in yt he useth filthy language to all sorts of people, ignorant in yt he wants learning and more good ness and yt he doth abound in wickedness

...And humbly pray ye remmoovall of him....'

The petition is signed by Robert Pleydell and his two sons, Lords of the Manor, and fifty-eight parishioners.

The vile vicar of Holyrood Omenie (Ampney Crucis today) was the evidently ill-named Benedictus Grace, who was given the living near Cirencester some three years prior to the public petition to have him removed. Charged with carrying a rapier, dagger and a 'javelyn', with which he threatened his parishioners, attacking a number with sticks, heaping contumely and abuse on others, and also 'lieing in wayt by highway, to affright his quiet and peaceable neighbors, scorning the warrants of Justice of peace, beating and wounding officers and living as lawless'. Furiously violent in conversation, hurrying over prayers and holding them at unreasonable times, he 'maliciously often abstracts himself at burials to vex his neighbors'.

Vexing his neighbours and conducting his personal

affairs in a scandalous manner might have held little sway on the church authorities of the day, but hearing that he 'denieth sacrament' to his parishioners brought a warrant from the Grand Committee for Religion, commanding the plaintiffs to testify in person against Benedict Grace 'hereof faill not at yt peril'. The vicar then pressurized his parishioners to testify in his favour. According to later evidence, 'he cunningly got our hand' and many certified that they were tricked into signing a document under false pretences but appealed 'to maintain our petition, humbly desiring that our ignorance may not be any barre to proceedings nor his cunning prejudice our innocence'.

Sworn statements and petitions against the choleric cleric heaped up. Most, as in this case of the two girls under the nut tree, were very specific.

'I Elizabeth Smith testifye that Benedc Grace vicar of Hollirood Ampney in the Countye of Glocr Came into the porch of the now dwelling house of Msr William Pleydall wheare I and Joan Clark stood arm in arms about ten of the Clock at night being very dark and asked us whether wee would goe to piss under the Nut trees, if we would that he goe with one of us at once and the other should stay behind till he had brought hir back with whom he went in place and then he leave hir and take the other and all this while did not only strive with us but at last pulled us apart and afterwards did put his hand under my apron and would have been very incivill but I got forth of his hand and ran away soe that he could not find me though he sought diligently for mee.'

Joan Clark testified in the same words as her friend, Elizabeth, but added '...as soone as I perceaved his intent I violently got forth of his hands with throwing myself against the wall and strooke my eye and made it black and blue which I wore a great while after and after he had left me I saw him hunt after and heard him ask for Elizabeth Smith'.

Avening Church, near Tetbury, owes its consecration to the Nuns of Caen in Normandy and Matilda, wife of William the Conqueror. Some claim it was built in penance for her unkind actions against Brictric of the Manor of Avening. He rejected a proposal of marriage from Matilda when he was emissary to the Flemish Court and was dispossessed of his lands and flung into jail for being so uncooperative in response to her approaches.

With monotonous regularity the graceless Grace was reported to be 'uncivill' with almost every female he encountered, despite the layering of petticoats, skirts and aprons.

A closer scrutiny reveals that Ampney was not an isolated case, but one of some two thousand parishes petitioning against the 'dumb dogs, ignorant drunkards, crawling vermin and popish dogs' serving them in canonical dress. Whatever scurrilous labels were attached to the unpopular vicar of Ampney, he was certainly not dumb — he counter charged the Puritan squire with a writ the following May, as did the neighbouring squire John Prettyman of Driffield, who was very highly connected with Royalist circles.

Whether the case was ever heard is uncertain; evidence shows that Grace was still ministering at Ampney in 1646 and, according to yet another complaint, still aggravating his neighbours. The Civil War, in which nearby Cirencester was well and truly embroiled, reverberated in religious circles and much of the church's affairs depended on the success or failure of the royal arms. From his meticulous entries Benedict Grace was still at Ampney Crucis in 1650, but appears as minister at Leafield in the eastern edge of the Cotswolds some two years later. He was, if nothing else, tenacious in his desire to make his mark at Ampney, for he was restored in his living there as the monarch was restored to the throne in 1660 and remained vicar of all three Ampney churches until his death in 1670.

Poverty

Penalty of the poor

Giving alms to the poor pre-dates the Scriptures and has continued in different guise throughout all history. Medieval merchants bequeathed their soul to the Almighty, a substantial endowment to 'ye moder churche' and charity in some form to their poorer neighbours. Such was the faith in the stability of the economic and social situations that such charity boards that are preserved in churches throughout the region, record that the alms were 'to continue for ever', as at Dymock Church.

The relief by charity from private benefactions and the church proved woefully inadequate by the time the Tudors had secured the throne at great national expense due to wars at home and abroad. Consequently, the great numbers of vagrants — caused by a combination of increased population, rising prices, the suppression of the monasteries and their ever-sought-after alms and sustenance to travelling poor, plus the extensive enclosure of arable land to spread the sheep pasture across the Cotswolds and resultant high unemployment — became a political issue. The Poor Relief Act of 1601 embodied Elizabeth I's earlier attempts to legislate a national system, but in effect relied heavily upon local interpretation and every parish had to provide a body of 'substantial householders' and churchwardens under the aegis of the Justices of the Peace as Overseers of the Poor.

A rate was levied on householders to raise some revenue towards the cost of supporting the poor in their parish. Support in reality meant ensuring that those that were poor were not so through their own fault of indolence. The Overseers were empowered to set able-bodied poor to work, the children as apprentices, and punished those who were unwilling to work at their designated tasks. The rate-payers also made their voice heard saying that they were not going to support the poor of other parishes and a Settlement Law was passed in 1662 to ensure their own parish would be chargeable should a stranger not work for his living or be able to pay his way.

Throughout the reign of William and Mary the poor were treated more like criminals than unfortunates. Those receiving parish relief were required to be 'badged' — a large red or blue 'P' on their right sleeve; the penalty for not displaying the badge of the pauper was instant withdrawal of relief, whipping in the stocks or a couple of weeks' hard labour in a House of Correction.

1714

To ye High Constable of ye Hundred of Long-tree [Tetbury] you are required with Petty Constables, Tythingemen and Overseers of the Poor at the Sign of the George in Stroud on the 6th day of January at ten of the clock in the morning to bring before us all persons that doo intrude into theyre parishes endeavouring to gayne theyre settlements there not being lawfully quallifyd; and all young unmaryed persons that doo live after an idle and disorderly manner and doo refuse to goe to service; and all poor children that they doe designe to putt to apprentice, and masters fitt to take them.

1880

Joseph Preston of Stow-on-the-Wold left his wife and went to live in London 'the wife therefore became chargeable on Stow Union from 1878 — Preston committed to Gloucester Prison for one month's hard labour'.

1880

A vagrant charged with sleeping rough in straw at Burford, therefore rendering it unfit for animal bedding, committed to prison for 14 days.

In the Churchwardens' accounts for Fairford an entry records that 'a stranger, who shall be called Charity — for having confessed to being a pauper from another parish but not able to produce his pass from that parish and not recovering from his malady in order to be returned to that parish, was given a pauper's funeral'.

The annuity from Robert Hale's charity at Wotton-under-Edge, by Deed dated 1578, of twenty shillings a year from land rent was to be distributed 'at the four usual feasts of the year amongst the poorest, most needy and impotent persons in the parish of Wotton, at the discretion of the Mayor and churchwardens, but not upon stout sturdy vagrant or counterfeit beggars or other poor person given to idleness, who if they would travail, might with the sweat of their own brows get their living'.

Plaque at Dymock Church: alms were to continue to be given to the deserving poor indefinitely.

Public penance

The powers for penalizing the poor and fallen were wielded in public in order that the whole parish was made aware of them.

1569 Estlache Marten

Alice Hatheway 'had a child the father of which is unknown. She confessed to the offence and said that William Mytche of Brodewey was the father. The judge (of Glos Consistory Court Office) enjoined her unto public penance in the parish church on the following Sunday and the Sunday following that'.

A typical workhouse: Fairford in 1817, called the House of Industry.

Nearly two centuries later, the vicar of the same church presented the following cases to the Bishop when he made his visitation to Cirencester in 1747.

> 'I baptised Reubin, son of Dorothy Allen of the Parish of East-Lech-Martin otherwise called Bouthrop; since therefore the churchwardens have not yet presented the said Dorothy (now the wife of Edmund Wheeler of the said Parish) for having a bastard child, I present her for the same. Also I present Anne Cock of the said Parish, widow, as lying under a common fame of fornication, which I verily believe to be upon just grounds, she being in all appearances big with child.'

The list of presentments included Joseph Small for not attending church for three months, and Thomas Sherborne, Clerk of the Parish 'for defamation and scandal in saying that I had wronged him'.

The Workhouse

The undeserving poor who had, under Elizabethan Poor Law, been disciplined and corrected in Houses of Correction, changed their habitat but not their status under George I, when parishes were empowered to build their own workhouses where 'the able-bodied might be employed and the children, the sick and the aged maintained'. If a place in the workhouse was refused, then parish relief was stopped. Whole families often ended up in the workhouse through illness of the breadwinner, unemployment or orphanhood. Fairford euphemistically named its workhouse The House of Industry; others more bluntly called it The Poor House.

In 1834 the new Poor Law brought about wretched conditions on the pauper children such as Charles Dickens immortalized in his *Oliver Twist*, when the emphasis was on greater 'efficiency' at the expense of compassion and humanity.

Schools of Industry made an abortive attempt to

start educating the poor children in useful arts fitting them for employment — and in fact, were little more than child home industries, as at Powells, Cirencester, known as the Yellow and Blue Schools, where 'the boys are to be bred up and instructed in the art of weaving worsted stockings' and the girls to spinning in 'a strong house'.

Dursley Workhouse, home to fifty-seven children between three and fifteen years of age in 1847, refused to dismiss its schoolmistress despite complaints that she taught only reading and sewing. The purpose of the workhouse, they stated, 'was to prevent destitution and starvation and not for education, however laudable it may be that a necessary proportion should be afforded even to the children of paupers'.

A reform of Parliament resulted in the revolutionary social step in 1834 of replacing the parochial system with Unions, under which a number of workhouses were administered by Guardians — twenty-three were set up in Gloucestershire. Little changed, except that the local freedom which had allowed some rare glimpses of humanitarian expenditure was often curtailed. The House of Industry at Fairford opened in 1773 and had twenty-three inmates by 1803; the men were employed 'to dig stones in ye Croft', the women were paid eight pence per pound to spin flax and sixpence per pound to weave sheeting. Barber Cowley received 6s 6d a year 'for shaving of ye old men' and Sarah Cowley had a new pair of whalebone stays costing 2s 6d. Between them, the inmates had 4s 3d to spend at the November fair. The rest of the annual thirty-seven pounds income, after paying the Governor's salary of fifteen pounds, was spent on a hundredweight of soap, a bushel of Epsom salts, pig-killing, funerals and tin cups.

In earlier times it was often converted buildings that served the purpose, as in Cirencester, until Lord Bathurst granted part of the Beeches in 1836 'provided the same can be done without inconvenience to

ARTICLES AND CONDITIONS TO BE OBSERVED BY THOSE POOR MEN AND WOMEN THAT ENJOY THE CHARITY OF HUGH PERRY E^{SQ} And ALDERMAN of LONDON

If any Persons in this Almshouse shall behave themselves in carriage or conversation as to be thought unfit & unworthy of the Charity of this Gift: then their part & portion of Apparel Fuel & Money shall be given to such Persons as the Mayor & his Brethren shall think fit. The persons enjoying this Charity shall constantly attend upon the Public Prayers at the time appointed for them to read. Those neglecting to attend on the Prayer shall be deemed as unworthy of the Charity aforesaid, which shall be distributed to other poor people as the Mayor and his Brethren shall think fit. That the lecturer should not be absent without the leave & consent of the Mayor. The Chapel shall be kept clean & decent by some one Almsman to be appointed by the Mayor who shall pay for the same. the poor scholars taught by the Gift are to be always present when the Prayers are read.

Articles and conditions still on display at the almshouse known now as Perry's Hospital in Wotton-under-Edge.

*Almshouses
at Burford.*

time at Gloucester Penitentary. Meat or fresh bacon was reserved for Sunday, then a meagre portion; potatoes and bread, gruel of oatmeal, salt, pepper and vegetable water, cheese and beer were apportioned out according to age and occupation. As with the dietary of lunatic asylums of the same period, washerwomen and those that worked in the gardens were allowed extra beer and snuff or tobacco. An amendment in 1836 to the dietary submitted to the Poor Law Commissioners from the Cirencester Union agreed that on five days a week 'the dinner of each adult shall be 1 lb potatoes that being the usual diet of the independent labourer in this district'. It was further resolved to divide the 5 ozs bacon allowed for Sunday between that day and Thursday 'thus affording two meat days without any additional charge to the ratepayer'. Such was the faith in the permanency of their edict, that the Guardians ordered the dietary 'to be framed and exhibited in the house'.

Christmas Day in the Workhouse

A report on Christmas Day at Northleach Workhouse in 1879 began by saying 'it was looked forward to by all inmates with pleasure ' — the text displayed over the chapel altar 'Come Unto Me' would not have tempted any, by choice, to the grim austerity of 'the house' on any other day of the year. What a relief to the monotony of the prescribed dietary must have been the 'plentiful supply of good old English fare of roast beef and plum pudding'. Beer, tobacco and snuff were doled out to the adults, and the children had the rare luxury of 'an orange and some sweets, which at the time seemed to make them forget their altered circumstances'. Similar festive fare was duly publicized for Tetbury, by the kindness of the Hon Mrs Whyte Melville, and for the workhouses in the Cirencester Union generally; a number even permitted 'innocent games' in the afternoon.

the neighbourhood'. A specially designed workhouse about 1860 at Cheltenham made provision for complete segregation of 'classes' as directed by the new law.

Segregation meant separation of families. Men and women had separate wards (sleeping dormitories) and day rooms, the boys and girls individual playground yards; a stone yard, workshop, laundry, bakehouse, drying ground and kitchen radiated from a central area on which stood the chapel. The Board room and office and waiting room flanked one side, school rooms ran from them to the chapel, and a yard for 'aged men' edged the boys' yard. A hospital yard, fever rooms for men and women separately, and a 'lewd

women's yard', overlooked by the chapel, led to the far end where the tramps had their own wards and exercise yard. The complex terminated with the Dead House, next to the Porter's Lodge. A little building marked on the plan as the 'Potato House' is shown close to the vegetable patch.

The dietary

Potatoes formed the major part of the workhouse diet, and the dietary was the subject of much discussion and amendment in a number of workhouses. Those at Cam, Uley, North Nibley and Dursley were shown to be poorer than the allowance for prisoners serving

An inside view from without

A Visiting Committee was formed in late Victorian times to report on the state and condition of workhouses within the Unions. Most reports were obviously slanted towards presenting a satisfactory picture to appease the authorities and ratepayers, but here and there can be spotted the frugality and futility of life and hope for an escape from the institutionalized system.

Life in the workhouse in 1890

1890 Cirencester Union

The children here, as at other workhouses, are almost all illegitimate. The orphans, twelve at present, are boarded out to the villages — one of the great obstacles is to those who remain that just as the matron and teacher are beginning to see an improvement, the mother comes to take them away and exposes them to all kinds of foul living, then brings them back again. We found everything spotlessly clean but very bare. The boys' dayroom has a stone floor, bare walls and two forms for furniture, the playground outside is equally bare. No pictures or playthings or games are anywhere to afford the slightest amusement. The chronic sick ward is bright with yellow quilts, gay pictures and flowers, but there should be a comb and brush for each bed — there is only one comb for the ward! In the nursery one pretty little mite was fast pining away and her mother, barely 23 and with two other children in the house, was helping in the kitchen with no shame at her position. In the kitchen the inevitable pea soup was being prepared. The average cost per head for maintenance and clothing is 3s 8½d per week. The lane outside is strewn with torn up tickets from tramps who obtain from the police a pass with his name, age and destination on it, which he hands to the Union, and on his leaving the master fills in the next house in the Union and where he might get bread. The employment is stone breaking, oakum-picking and gardening. A nut walk behind the front garden provides a pleasant promenade in the summer for the old people. The necessary house appeared to be badly situated and smelt offensively, a water closet or privy might be erected on the garden side of the ward.

There are no able-bodied males in the house, only infirm and old and a couple of casuals in the tramps' ward. There are no infectious cases in the fever ward, it was occupied on the male side only by one cripple boy. The inmates are understood to be healthy but the female children seem to be troubled with the itch, and were rubbing their limbs with hearthstone, but it did not appear to be through a fault of the master. The rules regarding schooling seem to be enforced, with the trifling exception of one boy who is not, but nearly quite, idiotic. Mostly, all looked clean and decently dressed.

Winchcombe about 1906 with the now-demolished workhouse centre top.

Extracts from the records of various workhouses. Discipline was strictly enforced with no remission, whatever the reason for breaking the rules.

Breaking the rules

1850

Winchcombe Union Workhouse

A tramp named John Fisher aged 59 years came for a night's lodging having obtained a ticket from the Relieving Officer. He was given 6 ozs of bread and directed to the tramps' sleeping ward. The next morning he was ordered to stone breaking when he complained he had no clothes to put on. The Master saw a heap of rags and asked Fisher if he had been tearing his clothes into bits; he said he did because they were so filthy and bad he could wear them no more. The Master sent for the police and after clothing Fisher with an old shirt, trousers and smockfrock, he was conveyed before the magistrate and committed to Northleach Prison to hard labour for 14 days.

1879

A man was charged at Tetbury for absconding from the workhouse wearing its uniform, having no clothes of his own. Committed to prison for 14 days.

1893

Three men were found guilty of refusing to execute a piece of work they had been ordered to do at Cirencester Workhouse, being casual inmates. The Master went into the yard and saw them doing nothing, yet they had the task of stone breaking. In an hour they had only produced a hatful. They said they could not as it was out of their line, and the 'stones were too much for any man'. They were committed for 10 days' hard labour, being told they would find the British taxpayers were not going to keep able-bodied men like them idle.

Reading the rules

1879

Advertisement for Nurse of Stroud Workhouse £20 per annum with board, lodging and washing. Must be single or widow without children and able to read the written directions of the Medical Officer.

More board than bed

The numbers returned for the Winchcombe Workhouse for the week ending 18 May 1850 showed that 'Beds Therein of the Old Men's Ward' were sixteen; the number of occupants each night of the week averaged twenty-five. Six beds in the Boys' Ward accommodated ten; only those in the Infirmary seemed to have the luxury of a bed each. Likewise in the Women's wards. Only the lying-in ward and Infirmary beds accommodated a single sleeper; most nights of that week able-bodied women had to share, and the girls had no less than three to a bed most nights.

Soup and sympathy

The desperate depression of the weaving communities around Chalford and Bisley prompted the vicar of Bisley, the Reverend Thomas Keble — brother of the poet divine, John Keble, to make a public appeal for donations to subsidize flour, potatoes and coals for the distressed families in 1837. Heading the list of subscribers with a personal donation of twenty pounds, Thomas Keble verified that many 'pass whole days without food' and numberless families had been compelled to part with furniture and clothing to provide a meal for their children.

Poverty was no newcomer to the weavers of the Stroud valleys. Robert Raikes had reported that at one Sunday School Treat at Painswick some half century before Keble's plea for help, one little boy could eat nothing. Having been without food at home for three days 'his stomach was gone'.

An Expedient to afford Substantial Relief of the Labouring People, by the substitution of other cheap, wholesome and nourishing food by means of soup establishments were offered to the Court of Quarter Sessions at Gloucester to reduce the consumption of bread corn.

The Reverend Thomas Keble, seen here with his wife, made and organized donations to help local poor families survive.

---

100 gallons of soup

by Winchester Measure, could be made from the following quantities, it was claimed.

112 lb legs and shins of beef
63 lb of clods and stickings
18 lb split peas or fresh vegetables
18 lb onions
30 lb barley
8 lb salt
10 ozs pepper

Using about $1\frac{1}{4}$ bushels of coals, the hundred gallons of soup could be made for £2 17s 3d. The recipe is lengthy, as is the cooking time — some seventeen hours of it — by which time, it is stated, the meat 'is nearly dissolved and only appears in particles or threads floating in the soup'. This is long after the initial rendering down of the bones and clods and stickings have sent 'the bloody and foul particles to float up and which can be skimmed off' before it is covered for the night to boil 'till six o'clock the next morning when the labourers return to take out the bones' — and then to continue to stir frequently to prevent sticking.

Another dish 'while it feeds the Poor in a cheap and nutritious manner', and, 'would be even prized at a rich Man's Table', the Suggestions continue, could be made by mashing white drum cabbages with potatoes using a part of the fat skimmed off the soup. This would work out to about a halfpenny per head. And, for a bonus, the report advocated that by teaching 'the Labouring People through this Method how good and palatable it is, they will resort to the same mode of dressing these Vegetables in their own Houses and thereby acquire better and more frugal Habits'.

The intelligence and zeal of Mrs Wilton, the cook at Cirencester Soup and Invalid Kitchen 'must not go unnoticed' the Honorary Secretary and Treasurer of the charity stated in his report of the 1879 account.

CIRENCESTER SOUP AND INVALID KITCHEN.

To the Editor.

Sir,—This useful charity has now existed for the last fourteen years, and it is so well known and so highly appreciated that it is unnecessary to advocate its claims to public support, which no doubt it will continue to receive.

The subscription list for the year ending 30th November last, amounted to £75 4s. 6d., being rather more than that for the two previous years, and the cost of providing for the kitchen was somewhat less than usual ; so that although we commenced the year with an adverse balance of £1 9s. 11d., we leave off with £1 11s. in hand,—a very encouraging result in these times.

Subscriptions for the ensuing year, viz., up to 30th November, 1880, may be paid to me as heretofore, for which tickets will be supplied at the rate of forty for a guinea, and in that proportion for any larger or smaller amount, from half-a-crown's worth upwards, and *at any time* during the year.

Due notice of the distribution of soup will be affixed at the door of the kitchen.

Subscribers are cautioned to see that the *soup* tickets given by them are used by the proper parties.

The invalid dinner and beef tea tickets for the deserving sick and needy, are almost certainly to be used correctly, and are of the greatest benefit to the poor recipients.

It only remains to add that the constant and judicious management of Mrs. W. Cripps—under whose watchful care this charity has now been carried on for the last 14 years—still continues unabated ; nor must the services of Mrs. Wilton, the cook, be unnoticed, who conducts the work entrusted to her with intelligence and zeal.

Statement of Receipts and Expenditure

	£	s.	d.
Amount of subscriptions received and tickets sold between 30th November, 1878, and 30th November, 1879	75	4	6
Pence received at the kitchen	11	0	9
	£86	**5**	**3**

	£	s.	d.		£	s.	d.
Balance due to Treasurer on 30th November, 1878	1	9	11				
Cost of materials for soup, invalids' dinners, and beef tea	59	10	4				
Wages of Mrs. Wilton, cook at the kitchen, for the year ending 30th November, 1879	21	9	0				
Fuel	1	12	0				
Printing	0	11	0				
Repairs to cooking apparatus ...	0	1	0				
Acknowledgment rent (Earl Bathurst allowing the premises to be used free of actual rent)	0	1	0		84	14	3
Balance in hands of Treasurer...					1	11	0
					£86	**5**	**3**

ROB. A. ANDERSON,
Hon. Sec. and Treasurer.
Cirencester, Dec. 19th, 1879.

A letter to the Editor in 1879 regarding the noted success of distributing soup, invalids' dinners and beef tea to the 'deserving sick and needy'.

Health and hospitals

Testimonial from the Rev. T. Hayes, Rector, Duntisbourne Abbots, near Cirencester.

Sir,—I have much pleasure in giving my testimony to the efficacy of your Anti-Dropsical Pills, which I have some time dispensed to the poor in my parish with the most beneficial effect.

I remain, yours faithfully,

Rectory, July 22nd, 1869.   THOMAS HAYES.

Hundreds of others.

Moore Cottage Hospital at Bourton-on-the-Water, named after its founder, the local philanthropist, George Moore, opened in 1861. It is the third oldest such institution in the country.

Fairford Cottage Hospital started literally in a small block of four cottages in Park Street in 1867, until a new site was given by the Lord of the Manor to build a purposely designed hospital to mark the Golden Jubilee of Queen Victoria in 1887. It is now the smallest hospital in the administrative county, despite having almost doubled in size since the Victorian red, hand-made, bricked building by Waller made its distinctive architectural statement in the old Cotswold stone-built market town.

Hospitals, like medicine and medical practice itself, have had a curious history. Having evolved from a kind of sanctuary or hospice for the sick and the poor to the sick and bad — bad because sickness was thought to be a kind of divine retribution, with disease the ultimate punishment for sin — they have appeared in various form since the Conquest. This notion was fostered in the building of leper hospitals outside the city walls of Gloucester, one at Tewkesbury in 1199 and St Laurence's at Cirencester, founded in the thirteenth century. So few such hospitals would indicate that the disease was not the scourge in the Cotswolds that it was in other parts of the kingdom.

Cirencester's other two hospitals of ancient foundation were St John's, founded by Henry II and St Thomas's in 1427, placed under the patronage of the weavers. Vestiges of their ancient past are preserved in the Transitional-Norman arcade of the Hall of the former in Dollar Street, and the Weavers Hall of the latter in Thomas Street, which must rank as the oldest secular building in the town. Born from the monastic ministrations to the sick and needy, who sought succour and rest on the long medieval pilgrimages, the parish church often became a sanctuary for the sick and the priest tended them as best he could; so early hospitals often followed the plan of churches with a broad nave for the patients and their progress watched from a raised dais. But it is only from the infirmaries and hospitiums of the monasteries that scrappy evidence can be traced and information discovered about the earliest form of hospital.

The very name hospital may have been derived from the hospitality they afforded, such as at Lechlade where the hospital of St John the Baptist was built in 1228 for the specific purpose of giving succour to the travellers at the important crossing on the Thames. A visitation by the bishop's clerk in 1290 records that 'regular discipline was in nowise observed, and it was ordained that among the brethren there should be uniformity of dress and in the colour of the same, and like uniformity in food and drink. Also that the dress of the sisters be accorded unto decency'. They were further forbidden to leave the precincts without licence and were accused of 'the vice of gluttony'. The reference to receiving the sick as

*Nursing staff and medical
board of Cirencester
hospital in the 1920s.*

well as weary is contained in the rule that a kind and courteous brother should be chosen to accord the hospitality 'for the sick received into the place'. Despite the ticking off from the bishop, things got even worse in the next decade and an inquisition was held in the parish church about the state of the hospital and, on hearing of 'enormities committed therein' several brothers, sisters, priests and laymen were expelled.

Stow-on-the-Wold had a medieval hospital founded 'by an Earl of Cornwall', but many hospitals were lost in the Dissolution although a great number had already fallen into disrepair or disuse from their original purpose when Henry VIII set about his drastic reform with moral vigour. Leland, his itinerant antiquary, jotted in his diary of the situation in the Cotswolds, when he visited the hospital in the ancient shire capital of Winchcombe, that, 'only the name of Spital remaineth'.

Priories and monasteries throughout the region, with their sizeable livings, were given as part and parcel of a manor to the Knights by the Plantagenets. The Knights Hospitallers set up their own hospitals across the Cotswolds — at Down Ampney an effigy of the knight who is said to have fought in the last Crusade lies in the church he helped the Order to build; at Quenington a magnificent gatehouse of the preceptory, under whose soaring arch Edward I must have rode when he held court there on his frequent visits to the area, stands sentinel to its past; Southrop and Meysey Hampton also had their benefices owned by the Hospitallers.

Temple Guiting preserves in its name its past connection with the Knights Templar, an opposing Order to the Hospitallers, to whom their lands were turned over when Edward II arrested the entire lot on orders of the Pope in 1308.

From their ties with monastery and manor, hospitals became the charitable object of merchant guilds and individual benefactors, such as those at Wotton-under-Edge. Perry's Hospital, founded in the early seventeenth century by Hugh Perry, a wealthy mercer, combined alms for six poor old men and six poor old women who were to be apparelled in gowns, shoes, stockings, shirts and smocks and provided with fuel and money as long as they behaved themselves 'in carriage and conversation' in the house built specially for them, with divine lectures by 'six worthy lecturers' and an usher 'to teach the youth in the free school'. Thomas Dawes left money in his will eighty years later which, at the discretion of the trustees, was used to erect a hospital 'for six poor persons or families and adjoining to a hospital in the said town endowed by one Mr Perry'. A General Hospital links the buildings into an attractive quadrangle more reminiscent of a miniature college than almshouse hospitals.

The term hospital was also applied to schools of industry. The Cotswolds had two such 'boarding hospitals', rare in England. The earliest was endowed by Thomas Webb in 1642, a Stroud clothier who left his house by the churchyard in which 'two honest poor widows' were 'to breed up four poor children' — a writer in 1709 reported that the boys were 'yearly clothed in red and thence called the Red Boys'. Their schoolroom was below the wool loft in the Market House until 1816.

At Cirencester, Mrs Rebecca Powell's charity bequest for a 'hospital school' had but a short life and became amalgamated with the Blue School founded by her husband.

Since their earliest times hospitals have been reliant to some greater or lesser degree on charity, patronage, alms — call it what you will. Many were built entirely on public subscription and financed by subscription and fundraising events until the National Health Service took them over.

Hospitals as we know them today have been a fairly recent public institution. The earliest record of one for

Early this century wheelchairs were rather grand affairs made of wickerwork. Fred Keylock is the injured party here, smiling despite a broken ankle.

the town of Cheltenham, for instance, which served the needs of the general public, was established in 1813 on a site which was then 318 High Street. A number of hospitals have fallen foul of economic policies and their closure leaves a deep wound in their community. The inauguration of a National League of Hospital Friends was formed soon after the great National Health Act of 1948, pre-empting the contin-

uing need for public awareness and support of our hospitals. The Hospital Sunday tradition dates back to 1873 as a consolidated effort which had been started in the previous century whereby church collections helped fund the upkeep of their nearest hospital, and throughout the Cotswolds the calendar is still punctuated with fetes and jumble sales and coffee mornings and carol singing and concerts for that very purpose.

Dr Charles Bloxsome, a motor-vehicle enthusiast as well as a medical practitioner, sets off on his rounds in a locomobile, a steam-driven car.

The Doctor

Samuel Tanner, shoemaker, was snatched from his grave to sell to London. The brothers Ashcombe (fictitious name) were caught and sent to Bisley lock-up and sent overseas to Botany Bay.

This 1938 report about body snatching in the *Wilts and Gloucestershire Standard* reads more like a paragraph from a Dickens novel, but medical practice had its dubious aspects until fairly late in civilized history. The 'Quacks Charter' as it became known was an Act of Parliament aimed at organizing the professions of physicians and surgeons, exempting from penalties those '... divers honest persons whom God hath endowed with the knowledge of the nature, kind and operation of certain herbs, roots and waters' — as long as they charged no fee other than for the herb itself.

It was in the reign of Henry VIII — a veritable biological challenge to any medical man — that surgeons were no longer required to act as barbers (the symbolic red and white striped pole of the barber being white bandages on blooded flesh), while barbers were confined under the Charter to restrict their surgical operations to dentistry. The Act also allowed the United Company of Barber-Surgeons to receive the bodies of four executed criminals each year for the dissection and study of anatomy.

A century and royal house later, James Vaulx had earned himself such a reputation in medical circles that James I summoned him to court that he might make him his own personal physician, but on enquiring how the doctor had reached such eminence in the art of healing and Vaulx explaining 'by practice', the canny Scot declined the temptation. 'By practice? Then by my soul thou shalt na' practise on me'. The great Dr Vaulx is portrayed with his two wives and sixteen children in the village church at Meysey Hampton, with an invitation to 'Stay, mortal' to read his epitaph in which he indicates that he 'bade men live when Nature bid them dye'.

The fame of Edward Jenner is vested in the Vale, but the wolds can claim to have 'schooled' him at Wotton-under-Edge and Cirencester. Cheltenham, known as 'the gateway to the Cotswolds', housed his first vaccination clinic in the Georgian villa called Alpha House, promptly renamed The Pest House.

Another Cotswold doctor who made his mark in medicine through the pox and pestilence of the day was Thomas Dover, grandson of the Robert Dover who instituted the Cotswold Olympics — today his name lives on only in the Dover's Powder for diarrhoea. His tomb at Stanway where he was buried in the Tracy vault was destroyed during the renovations at the turn of the century.

Dr Thomas Dover, nicknamed Doctor Quicksilver from his revolutionary cure by metallic mercury for the treatment of venereal disease, invested his not inconsiderable fortune in legalized piracy, known as 'privateering', and surprised everyone by declaring that he was taking the captaincy of the second ship engaged in an enterprise during the Spanish Succession. The remarkable outcome of the venture was that it was Dover who commanded his crew to land on the largest of the Pacific Islands in search of fresh vegetables as there was an outbreak of scurvy on board. It was there, on a supposedly deserted island, that they found Alexander Selkirk who had been marooned for four years and four months. It is therefore to the venturesome spirit of Doctor Dover that literature owes the immortal classic *Robinson Crusoe*. Dover's own book, *The Ancient Physician's Legacy to His Country*, may not have endured as long as Defoe's novel, but its eight editions were translated into French, and from one of the references is evidence that an outbreak of typhoid fever struck the Cotswolds in 1728-29 when Doctor Dover was 'called to several houses where eight or nine persons were down at a time'.

It was not until the last century that surgeries as such were set up by doctors in the community — hitherto either the doctor visited the patient at home, or as in medieval times, the 'leeches' were attached to private households only. Surprisingly, it is to Tsarist Russia one has to go to trace the oldest comprehensive Health Services when in 1862 teams of doctors were designated a round of visits to rural areas; the whole community then were compelled to visit him en masse. Research points to Bismarck's Germany as being the inspiration for Lloyd George's National Health Insurance scheme but it was two world wars later before the National Health Service was set up.

The family doctor is still very much a part of the Cotswold community and has always commanded a reverent respect. His very word is cherished as creed and gospel, to be repeated and obeyed. A doctor friend of mine summed this up when telling how he had been called out to a patient, carefully wrote out the prescription with the strict instructions that the ailing husband was to take half a wineglassful of the medicine twice a day. On his next visit the doctor was more than a little affronted to find that the old man had not improved and the medicine bottle unopened stood on the mantlepiece. 'That be the trouble, doctor,' the old lady replied, quite distressed. 'I got the physick as you said from the chemist, but I couldn't buy half a wineglass not nowhere.'

Holloway's Ointment, it was claimed, could cure all manner of ills, from diptheria to gout!

A Certain Cure for Bronchitis, Diphtheria, Sore Throat, Asthma, &c.

For curing sore throat, diphtheria, bronchitis, asthma, tightness of the chest, and pain in the side—which instant treatment alone prevents degenerating into more serious maladies, this Ointment has the same powers over chest complaints as a blister possesses, without causing pain or debility. Old asthmatic invalids will derive marvellous ease from the use of this Ointment, which has brought round many such sufferers and re-established health after every other means had signally failed.

Bad Legs, Bad Breasts, Old Sores, and Ulcers.

By rubbing the Ointment round the affected parts, it penetrates to the tissues beneath, and exercises a wonderful power on all the blood flowing to, and returning from, the diseased part. The inflammation diminishes, the pain becomes less intolerable, the matter thicker, and a cure is soon effected. In all long-standing cases, Holloway's Pills should also be taken, as they will thoroughly expel all depraved humours from the body.

Gout, Rheumatism, Stiff Joints.

Gout and Rheumatism arise from inflammation in the parts affected. To effect a permanent cure, adopt a cooling diet, drink plenty of water, take six of Holloway's Pills night and morning.

The dentist and the district nurse

'We didn't have a dentist when I was a boy. I remember having toothache so bad once my father gave me sixpence to go to old Mr Manning, the chemist, to have it out. He sat me in a chair in the kitchen, tied a length of string to my tooth, tied the other end to the door knob, said "look at me my bwoy", then kicked the door to — out came my tooth. When I got home my father said, "Well, we could have done that ourselves and saved our sixpence" — and that's what we did.'

Pop Morse's recollections of his dental treatment in the 1890s sparked off memories of George Swinford's childhood in Filkins. 'My dad gave me sixpence to have my tooth out at the vet's — we didn't have a 'pothecary in the village, but I spent it on a penknife and my toothache got better somehow. Anyway, I haven't got the tooth now, but I've still got my knife'.

England had marched to war against Germany before the first clinic was opened in Stroud and the School Dentist became a figure in his own right. Shortly before the Care Committee made dental care in children one of their remits in 1914, Sir Philip Stott at Stanton in the north Cotswolds, and the Duchess of Beaufort at Badminton in the south, had set up small clinics in their villages. It was the greatest stride forward in that field for a thousand years, during which time dentistry of sorts had been carried out by barbers and blacksmiths, vets, midwives, wheelwrights and apothecaries (the poor man's doctors) and anyone else with a strong wrist and sufficient insensitivity. But no sooner had the service started at Down Ampney School than 'The First World War took away the dentist and the nurse has pulled the teeth of several children with their parents' consent'.

The District Nurse, first on her creaking sit-up-and-beg bike, later in her Baby Austen, has been bringing folks into this world and laying them out ready for the next between the days of Mrs Gamp and the recent

'A pretty little place,' said the Duke of Connaught, visiting one of his troop injured while on manoeuvres in the town in 1909. The family of J Arthur Gibbs (author of A Cotswold Village *) made a donation in his memory which enabled the extension on the right to be built.*

The foundation stone for Fairford Cottage Hospital, the smallest in Gloucestershire, was laid in 1887 — on the site of the old workhouse.

As Matron, nurses and patients pose for the camera, the patients prepare to enjoy a wireless set donated by the Women's Institute in 1928.

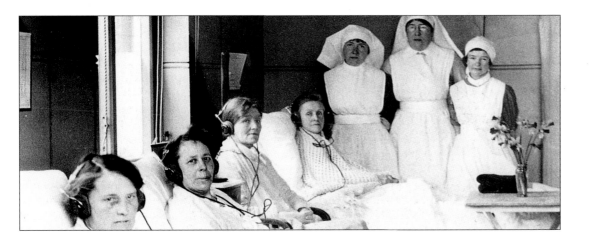

Two open-ended south-facing verandas were added in 1933. Today voluntary donations and fund-raising — through the League of Friends — is still the hospital's major source of support.

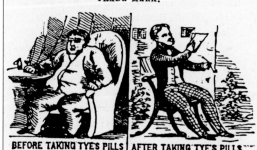

Mrs Betty Smith, a district nurse in Colesbourne in about 1909 with her regulation bicycle.

'Before and after' illustrations underline the great claims made for Tye's pills.

TYE'S DROPSY, LIVER, & WIND PILLS.
TRADE MARK.

BEFORE TAKING TYE'S PILLS | AFTER TAKING TYE'S PILLS

IF you are suffering with Dropsy and wish to be CURED lose not an hour in procuring a Box of these most Wonderful Pills. They will cure you as surely as you take them. They give immediate Relief in Sick and Nervous Headache, Wind in the Stomach and Bowels; remove the Bile, assist Digestion, cure Costiveness, Giddiness, Sickness, Palpitations, and Nervous Complaints. As a Liver Pill they can have no rival, being composed of the most powerful Vegetable Extracts, which have direct action on the Spleen and Liver, and the happy effect of which can be seen after one or two doses. TYE'S DROPSY PILLS act like a charm in the Cure of Asthma, Bronchitis, Influenza, and every description of Coughs and Colds; they are rapidly taking the place of every other remedy, and only need a trial to recommend themselves to every household in the land. For testimonials, &c., see hand bills. The Dropsy Pills are sold in Boxes at 1/1½, 2/9, 4/6, and 11/- each. Sent under cover to any address on receipt of stamps, by the Proprietor, J. Baxter, Chemist, Kingstanley, Gloucestershire.—Sold in CIRENCESTER by C. H. SAVORY, Stationer, W. Griffiths, J. Paternoster, and J. W. Mason; Stroud, R. Barrett; Swindon, E. R. Ing and W. J. Smith; New Swindon, S. J. Smith; Chippenham, J. C. Coles; Sherston and Corsham, Neal and Sons; Cricklade, W. Hayward and W. Golding; Ashton Keynes, J. Brain; Malmesbury, J. Witton and W. Brown; Wootton Bassett, G. Watts; Tetbury, Mr. Walker, and by Chemists everywhere. London wholesale agents, Sutton, Barclay, Sangers and Butler, and Crispe; Birmingham, Southall Brothers and Barclay.

Testimonial from the Rev. T. Hayes, Rector, Duntisbourne Abbots, near Cirencester.

Sir,—I have much pleasure in giving my testimony to the efficacy of your Anti-Dropsical Pills, which I have some time dispensed to the poor in my parish with the most beneficial effect.
I remain, yours faithfully,
Rectory, July 22nd, 1869.   THOMAS HAYES.
Hundreds of others.

restructuring of the domiciliary services. The Nurse, to generations of country people, implies the District Nurse who 'knows every one of her babies', the visiting comfortable figure in her navy-blue raincoat: confidante, mother confessor and medical mentor since she was conjured out of the infamous nursing ranks by

Florence Nightingale's reforming disciples in 1857.

She also appeared in the Stroud area as an experiment scheme for 'school medicals', and quickly came to be dubbed 'Nitty Nora' as she probed the heads of squirming school children to fill in the official returns of how many were 'dirty, verminous, or clean'. Her findings on one occasion in the village of Bibury, and the subsequent action wrought with vengeance by 'the lady and her gardener from the Big House' on an evacuee who was reported to 'be quite alive' nearly started another war.

My own memories of my Nurse was marvelling at her discretion and diplomacy. Privy to the neighbourhood's secrets, which she kept close to her bosom and locked in her mysterious commodious black bag, she was being 'pumped' one day on the purpose of her visit to a young lady's house and replied, 'Well, all I can say is that she isn't as she was, but she wouldn't have been as she is if she hadn't been no better than she should be'.

Peddling pills with carrying the news to rural areas was an age-old trade and every fair and market had its mountbank and quack doctor expounding the virtues of their cures. A wide audience was reached with the coming of newspaper publication and their advertisements. Widow Welch was praising the power of her

1735

Cure for the Deaf by Mr Ducket, an approved operator for the Hearing who (by the Blessing of God) hath found out Medicines that cure all sorts of Deafness, or Noise in the Head or Ears, if curable, as testified by Hundreds of People several of Whom hath been Deaf since their Cradle. He cures Persons of all ages at the House or Lodging of such Persons without Pain or Confinement or Hindrance of Business.

1874

Dental surgery. Artificial teeth fitted without extraction or springs.

Female Pills in 1879 while, with some indifference on the part of the typesetter, Dr Tye's Dropsy, Liver and Wind Pills and Stiff's Starch appeared to have exactly the same attributes! Meanwhile, in the *Wilts and Gloucestershire Standard* bee stings were being advocated as the best remedy for rheumatism.

Thomas Powell, known locally as Doctor Powell on account of his being an apothecary — not to be confused with grocers who also sold patent medicines — favoured the personal approach in 1890 by sending his customers a little Bouquet Almanack in which they were reminded that Powells Fairford Corn and Wart Cure cured not only those of local people 'but also those of people farther afield', testified by a letter from a grateful Headmaster at Tetbury. His range of pills and potions was extensive and could claim to cure everything from gripe to fits: artificial limbs and sea-going chests (presumably for medicine!) jostled for attention with rose dentifrices, insect powder, tinctures of myrrh and borax, Western Hunt sauce, pomades and sedative creams, podophyllin pills (replacing mercury); not forgetting Powells Great Bitter Tonic of quinine and dandelion 'to purify the blood and give tone and vigour to the frame'.

Prescriptions were sealed in envelopes and medicines wrapped in brown paper and sealed with wax. The collecting of 'physick' for the old people of an outlying village provided a fairly lucrative errand service for the young; missing school 'to go to the doctor's' was admissable and if the doctor was espied entering the village on his rounds there was a veritable scuffle among those willing to hold his horse for sixpence, and the bonus of some hot manure for the garden for nearby neighbours if his calls were lengthy.

A local pharmacy's prescription envelope: front and back.

No. 31260

The Prescription.

Mrs Evans

Dispensed by

Manning & Son

(F. W. Manning, M.P.S.),

Dispensing & Family Chemists,

Park Corner Pharmacy, Fairford.

DEPÔT FOR UCAL MEDICAL

Products & Toilet Requisites.

Prescriptions compounded from the Freshest and Purest Drugs. Accuracy and Skill are assured if you always take your Prescriptions to a

"UCAL" CHEMIST.

The Club

'... a certain disciple named Tabitha, which by interpretation is called Dorcas; this woman was full of good works and alms deeds which she did... and all the widows stood by him weeping, and shewing the coats and garments which Dorcas made, while she was with them.'

Acts IX gives us the origins of the Dorcas Society which was so active in Victorian times whereby good ladies of the parish raised funds by subscriptions for materials which they then made into shifts and necessaries for the poor. At Winchcombe, where the rules for the local society are preserved, there is a notice that in 1832 'tale-bearing and frivolous conversation' was fined one shilling.

Charles Dickens wrote that there was a society for just about every cause imaginable, but mutual benefit clubs can be traced back to the Romans; medieval guilds instituted their own related to trades and professions to help members who fell on hard times through sickness or bereavement. It was the drastic depression and deprivation caused by the Industrial Revolution which highlighted the poverty that erupted in Victorian times, and that is the age which fostered the founding of such a plethora of benefit and mutual assistance clubs in the Cotswolds.

The Club was the corporate term for the societies operating under wonderful names like The Ancient Order of Foresters, The Buffaloes, Odd Fellows, Druids, Hearts of Oak and Friendly Society. The principles were the same — that of giving financial

---

Female Friendly Society Rules

1st July 1839

The meeting to be held at Mr Thomas's house will explain the benefits of ensuring 5 shillings per week during sickness for single and married females of Fairford arising from indiscretion. Also to married females, 6 shillings per week during the lying-in month. Open to working persons and domestic servants not receiving £6 per annum. No one actually labouring under sickness shall be admitted as a member without the payment of 5 shillings in addition to the membership fee. Age limit 18 - 50 years. Sick members will be visited to prevent imposition.

---

assistance on a pension basis during sickness and at old age; benefits varied in dividing the surplus funds; many clubs followed the scheme spearheaded by George Holloway of Stroud and, taking his name to form the nucleus of the most successful societies in the Cotswolds, are still running today. In the history of the Cirencester Benefit Society — which began its useful life in 1890 under the title of The Cirencester Conservative Association Working Men's Benefit Society — Mary Bliss and Mary Day searched the records to find that Sir Thomas Davies, its chief secretary for forty-six years, had paid for a bed at Weston-super-Mare and that it had in 1926 'been occupied by 3 women and 9 men'. The authors added their own comment on this: 'presumably not all at the same time'!

For many years benefit societies were set up as separate clubs for men and women.

To 'be on the Club' imposed its own rules in the neighbourhood and many is the tale of such visitations because a member was seen carrying a basket or fetching water from the village pump, on the premis that if he was fit to be doing that he was fit enough for work so must 'be swinging the leg'. In a number of society rules there was the 'curfew' clause, that a member was not to be seen out of doors after dark.

An early form of advertising the benefits of the mutual assistance societies was the great Club Walk or Outing, when the Lodge banner was proudly carried aloft, accompanied by the local band. Aimed at recruiting new members, Club Days soon found their honoured place in the social calendar when the whole village would turn out in their Sunday best to take part in the gentle junketings.

The rules of an Amicable Society of 1814 would only allow membership of those who had cow pox or smallpox innoculations. Attendance of a member at another member's funeral was rewarded with 4d from the society's funds; no doubt this swelled the ranks of the mourners considerably!

The Club Day outing:
Sherborne in 1920.

Law and order

'…the brooke to be rydde by the Sunday after St Peter's days'

This law passed by Northleach Court Leet, the only Leet to survive in the Cotswolds, was an early form of pollution control of the River Leach on which the ancient wool-trading town stands. Not only were the townsfolk of 1578 ordered to make sure their water supply was free of debris, but anyone found washing in the Leach was fined fourpence.

Quaint and curious are some of the old customs linked to the medieval laws of the Court Leet —whose survival is due to the considerable efforts and support of the Earls of Bathurst. One of the duties of the High Bailiff and Trustees was that of ale-tasting, dating back to 1576 when ale was a penny a gallon. For this a white coat had to be donned, known on the Cotswolds as a 'Burford Moon' and ale-houses which sold food were open to inspection: a record of this ancient health and safety measure states 'Ye first time we went to Mistress Westwood's where we received chicken and wine'. The convivial nature of the inspection led to one member being ordered to remain sober and guide his companions safely home. The scale of the wealth and influence of the administrative body of the law in Northleach can be judged by their being the owner in 1619 of the Great House which became the first Sherborne Arms public house. Issuing licences for the selling of ale, raising and administering money for charitable purposes, relieving the poor and keeping the almshouses in repair, were additional responsibilities to the keeping of law and order in the locality.

The village constable

The village bobby on his bike is a fondly held memory of a not-so-recent past and many a tale has been told of his homespun law in the order of things in the community. 'It takes a rogue to catch a rogue' was an oft-quoted saying, with a nod and a wink, for it was the bobby who knew the local poacher and his habits and, if tales be true, always had a plump cock pheasant for his own pot, charming the bird out of the tree with his special issue powerful torch.

The office of village constable dates back a thousand years. In Saxon times the post derived from 'marshal of the stables'. The Normans merely shuffled the order of things around a bit, finding the system was working, but compelled to make it their own by adapting the tithing of ten men to become a territorial unit and made the chief of the tithing the constable.

Courts and punishments: corporal and capital

To be 'taken up the steps' is a local term describing being taken to Court. It stems from the fact that so many of the court houses or magistrates' courts were raised from the ground, albeit sometimes by only one or two steps, but in many cases on another storey.

Sometimes, as at Stow on the Wold, rewards were drawn up on a local scale to attract information leading to a conviction. At a meeting at Lower Swell, an adjacent village, it was decreed in 1810 that these should be as follows:

Rewards for information
Highway footpad robbery 4 guineas
Stealing a horse 3 guineas
Stealing wood 1 guinea
Stealing turnips a half guinea

A writer in the *Gloucestershire Countryside* in the early 1940s recorded that he had met a man who had witnessed a woman being publicly whipped for stealing wood from a hedge — obviously she did not have the means to pay the heavy, for those days, fine.

School groups re-enact Cotswold life of earlier times in the precincts of the old prison at Northleach.

A cursory search through the court cases of the last century underlines the old maxim 'God helps him who helps himself, but God help him as gets caught'.

1837

Robert Saunders, aged 41, burglariously broke open the dwelling house of Mr John Webb of Stroud and stole two ends of woollen cloth — transported for 15 years.

1862

George Jones, a carter at Ampney, fined 10/6d for driving a wagon drawn by three horses without reins.

1879

Edward Sharp of Tetbury stole two rabbits — ten days' hard labour.

William Hinton committed for six months' hard labour for procuring a pair of boots from Mrs Emma Giles at Fairford on false pretences. The defendant was found to be wearing the boots when Mrs Giles was attracted to their squeaking while at divine service at which Hinton was ringing the church bells.

(Which bears out the old saying that if your shoes squeak it means they're not paid for!)

1880

At Nailsworth a man was imprisoned for two months for stealing two fowl at Christmas.

A man who stole meat from the Bull Hotel at Fairford was hissed all the way to the court by the townspeople.

Harmer, a mason of Eastleach, who stole a vest from the Swan Inn and pledged it for a shilling at a Lechlade pub was sentenced to 14 days' hard labour.

1881

Prainy Cross, a tramping woman, was found to be drunk at Fairford, given 7 days' hard labour.

Edward Lydiard, labourer, brought up in custody at Malmesbury as being the bailee of half a crown given him by mistake for a penny in payment of cockles in the town on the evening by Ernest Bartlett; charge withdrawn when Lydiard refunded the half a crown.

At the same hearing Henry King, draper of Malmesbury, summoned for not having his child vaccinated according to the law, fined £1 with 7 shillings cost.

1929

Fined half a crown and bound over to keep the peace at Fairford — Charlotte Westbury for drenching with dirty chamber water Ellen Maud Cowley at East End cottages.

The ancient Court House Inn at Oakridge retained the name of its origins. Gruesome in detail, its room of execution with a cross beam 'hard as iron it took two men a whole day with a two-handled saw to cut it down', a waiting room where the condemned waited out their last hours, an adjacent small room with a window so that a watcher could make sure the body was not snatched 'to be sold for science', and an inbuilt stone basin 'where the Judge would wash his hands' were still in evidence, bearing witness to a hard past, as the country prepared to fight the Second World War.

The House of Correction:
Northleach prison.

Sanctuary

Seeking sanctuary in church as a means of escaping with one's life, was taken advantage of at least twice at Dursley. Our forefathers' sense of drama was well played out there in the instance of one of Lord de Berkeley's servants who, in 1221, was accused of killing a woman — records do not state whether by accident or design. The fellow escaped his captors and fled to Dursley church, confessed his crime and was pardoned on the condition he 'abjured the realm'.

Banished for ever from his home town, his sentence was read out in the church porch under a wooden cross held above his head and 'ungirt, unshod, bareheaded and in his bare shirt' he was ordered to make his way to the nearest port, presumably Bristol, and straightway walk into the water up to his knees to show his intent of leaving the English shores as soon as he could get ship to take him.

Two hundred years later a John Barbour, said to be of Cirencester, stole a horse from a Tetbury tailor and made off with it — the tale has it that it was to get to Bristol to run away to sea of his own accord — conscripting the help of the horse. When the hue and cry was raised and tracked him down at Dursley, the said John Barbour threw himself on royal mercy and Henry VI 'out of pity pardoned the said felon' and he walked out of the church a free man.

Justice — rough and ready

'Yes, I be turned sixty but never been to Gloucester by meself. You'll think me a bit of a coward, but I knows I couldn't do it. But [brightening up] if they wanted to cut a man's yud off, I reckons as I could hold it for 'em.'

It was certainly with a great degree of sadistic satisfaction that our forefathers — and mothers and their innocent little offspring — watched a public display, of humiliation at least and barbaric suffering at worst, in the course of seeing justice done. It was regarded as a kind of treat for the children to witness a hanging and specially inscribed bobbins commemorating the most infamous felons' despatch were a prized souvenir dangling on many a matron's lace pillow.

Most parishes had their own gallows on a triangular patch, usually where roads met near the parish boundary. Records for Sheepscombe in the sixteenth century speak of a William Motley holding free tenancy of a portion of land for the services of 'constructing the gallows, maintaining a ladder, and acting as Tithingman'. Local legend points to a place known as Jack's Green as the deadly spot.

But it is the home of the hangman which sends the shivers down sensitive spines. Eerie enough in its isolation, an old house which is perched on the edge of Painswick parish hides its secret behind tangled trees, its structure a skeletal shape as a result of years of neglect; time and clime have ravaged its roof and picked away at its stonework like an invisible carrion. Glassless windows stare out like sunken sockets towards Ticklestone Lane and a glance at the map confirms that this is The Haunted House, haunted enough to warrant a title as such.

The fearless phantom seeker may venture forth and get as far as the door and there notice a date — 1689. This, according to the oft-told tale is when the hangman set out as usual to perform his grisly task

The Gibbet Tree at Burford
where highwaymen were hung.

before dawn cracked across the valley. A number of sheep-stealers had to be dealt with and as on such occasions an assistant was employed; the hangman just got on with the job. It was not until the hood was removed from one of the bodies as they were loaded into a cart that the tragedy was discovered. It is said, with much solemnity and head-shaking as befits the sorry tale that, eager to witness a real hanging, the gallowsman's son had crept out, followed his father from the house, hidden under the gallows and there was mistakenly taken by the assistant as one of the number to be executed. Hooded, as the others, in rough sacking and with his hands tied behind his back, he met his untimely and horrific end at the hands of his own father — who, on finding the truth on his return home, hanged himself from a beam in the house.

The Gibbet Tree a couple of miles beyond Burford, near Capps Lodge, still stands today, gnarled and crooked branches reach out of the old oak like a witch's fingers pointing to the sky. Witness to the days of the dashing and notorious highwaymen, the stout oak held the bodies of two of the most infamous of them, Tom and Dick Dunsden who, with their brother Harry, terrorized the neighbourhood 'with divers robberies on the King's highway'. Encased in stout bands of iron, the Dunsdon brothers attracted a steady crowd of onlookers for as long as they were displayed after being hanged at Gloucester gaol in 1784. No doubt the landlord at Capps Lodge Inn, who had survived a direct shot from one of the gang, made the most of the story and the increased trade as the eighteenth-century day trippers tripped across the field to gaze upon the 'desperate fellows', safe in the knowledge that they could no longer draw a pistol, then back to the inn to hear at first hand how it was that mine host escaped death by the halfpenny piece being in his breast pocket and deflecting the bullet. It is said that his daughter wore the red plush waistcoat with its bullet hole for the rest of her life.

Stocks and lock-ups

They say that he that sups with the devil must have a long spoon, but in the Cotswolds it was more a case of she who has a wayward spouse must have a long-spouted teapot....

The old village lock-ups were tiny buildings. Windowless, they became known as 'blind houses', and were designed for the drunks and disorderly, poachers and general disturbers of the peace rather than true felons. The little stone-built and stone-tiled lock-up at Bibury stands close to the Swan Hotel and is in good preservation. The one at Filkins is now part of the small folk museum, housed in a couple of cottages; of the Burford lock-up only the door remains. Their common feature is the small round holes in the stout door. Designed for a peephole for the constable and a token attempt at air circulation for the confined, the holes became the means by which prisoners received morsels of food from their good wives. Even better was the devoted spouse who would go to the inn and have her teapot filled with beer and poke the spout through one of the holes so that her husband could just get his mouth round it and have the beer poured in. It is said that then the men went to meet their magistrates in good heart, and it was the only food and drink they received whilst confined in the blind house.

Bisley lock-up, bearing a date stone of 1824, is a very public two cell-affair and an ornate architectural feature with its ogee pitched roof and stone finial.

The stocks at Burford stood with the whipping post and the cross close by the Tolsey, where tolls were paid and the town's market transactions were carried out. The Tolsey is now a Parish Council meeting place and houses an interesting local museum. Winchcombe's heavy wooden stocks are a curiousity, now nicely preserved under a neat stone-tiled roof — a facility denied the unfortunates who were clamped and cramped into them sitting on a hefty rough hewn

Bibury lock-up: these windowless little buildings were known as 'blind houses'.

Wooden stocks on the village green at Stow on the Wold.

Ornate Bisley lock-up had two cells side by side.

timber. The seven-holes design is unique in the Cotswolds and, according to local lore, was built to accommodate three felons and a troublesome one-legged scallywag.

Old records in the North Cotswolds also speak of payments made to dog-whippers; these were church officials whose duties included keeping dogs under control in church in the days when farmers and shepherds took their dogs with them, before the Dog Tax was introduced in 1796. Some evidence also explains the height and close-railed design of altar rails so 'that doggs may not gett in'. The ancient poppy-head pew ends in Stanton church are gouged with chains from shepherd dogs who endured many a long sermon at their master's side.

Looking for all the world like a pair of pince-nez, the 'Squire's specs' stocks at Painswick were made in 1840, no doubt by the local smith, and were used for twenty-one years.

Just deserts

There is many a Hangman's Stone or Bridge in the Cotswolds — these are not public execution sites, but have been woven into the fabric of folklore as a salutory warning to would-be thieves. Their name springs from stories of a sheep-rustler who led his living loot along the road on the end of a rope. Tired, he sits down on a bridge or stone perched above a drock. The approach of someone in the dark sets the rustler hastily to conceal the sheep. Having wound the rope round his neck he lets the sheep down behind him, not realizing the depth of the drop the other side. The sudden weight of the falling sheep hangs the thief and the gallowsman is cheated out of another dawn job.

Divine retribution

An extract from a journal dated 1796 points to the risk run by those bent on disturbing a divine service.

The Reverend William Bishop of Gloucester began to deliver a weekly lecture but had no sooner commenced the service than an attempt was made to interrupt him by the mistress of the next house. She procured a fiddle and held a country dance, the noise of which was kept up upon the same floor, and within four or five feet of the preacher, so near were the houses. On the next day, a very striking event happened; this woman was taken ill in the morning and a corpse at night.

More graphically cast is the warning sculpted on the tomb of Perrott, the Cam farmer who broke the Fourth Commandment in 1685. The farmer figure is shown ploughing — tradition has it that this dastardly deed was done on a Sunday when he should have rested from his labours in accordance with the Holy Book. Judgement was swift. The chain by which the horses drew the plough snapped and flew back to hit the feckless farmer on the head, causing his death.

In clink

1790
Dietary for those on hard labour,
atrocious males and idle apprentices and
servants:
one and a half pounds of bread a day and twice
weekly one pint of soup made from coarse but
wholesome meat, peas or other vegetables.
Non-hard labour prisoners can receive
additional food from friends.

In the late eighteenth century there were Houses of Correction at Cirencester and Winchcombe. In the former the men's cell was a single room sixteen by eleven feet, with a women's cell above; in the latter, prisoners were kept in the cellar until two garrets fourteen feet square were put into use, but as the roof and floor met, the highest point in which the prisoners could stand was in the middle. Confined to their cells, they were without straw to sleep on and many had been put in irons to retain them as the yard was deemed inadequately secure in 1776. The eighty-year-old keeper had a licence to sell beer to the inmates.

It was against the background of such reports and the pioneering work of the Gloucestershire prison reformer, Sir George Onesiphorus Paul, that the Tudor bridewell system by which prisoners should not idle their sentence away but be put to good use, came about. In consequence Northleach Prison was built and another at Horsley.

Northleach bridewell was designed with yards radiating from the central unit in which the keeper resided. Sleeping cells were an innovation and measured the same six by seven feet as the work cells. Separation of prisoners was considered the only way of restricting contamination by way of disease, illness and lewd habits. It served a committal area of nine magistrates' courts and incorporated the dreaded treadmill which could be worked by seven men at a time. Statistics relating the time men over fourteen years were put to work the treadmill estimate that in a nine-hour session each man would have stepped on the eight-inch slatted treads the equivalent of climbing Gloucester Cathedral tower forty-six times.

An insight of those days is now an important educational facility as Northleach Prison houses the award-winning Countryside Collection as well as the magistrate's court, cells and equipment which can be seen *in situ*.

*W.P.C. Edith Lodge
joined the police force
in 1927.*

From stocks to cashmere stockings

When I joined the Police Force in 1927 the older men frowned on us and thought we should be indoors by ten o'clock; we were made fun of by the cartoonists in our navy blue tunics, with the skirt an obligatory ten inches from the ground, black high-legged boots and black cashmere stockings. All this was surmounted by a heavy black hunting hat.

WPC Edith Lodge (later Mrs Yeoman) recalled her early days as one of the county's first policewomen — Gloucestershire having the second oldest police force in the country. It was also one of the first to engage women in its service — and the innovator of women police motor-cyclists.

The move from local rough justice whereby minor offenders were put in the village stocks to the sophisticated service and legal proceedings of today was slow, ponderous and very parochial. Parishes had their beadle and watchmen and constable – the watchmen, under the law of Charles II, come down through history, according to contemporary reports, as:

'...chosen from poor, old decrepit men, who from their want of bodily strength, are rendered incapable of getting a living by work. These men, armed with no more than a pole – which few can scarcely lift – a bell, lantern and rattle, are to secure the persons and houses of His Majesty's subjects from the attacks of young, bold, stout, often desperate and well-armed villains'.

Although the vale towns of Cheltenham, Bath, Gloucester and Worcester had their own police force, by the time of Sir Robert Peel's Constabulary Act of 1839, the need for a county-covered force was sparked off by the riots in the Cotswolds cloth-making valleys of the Stroud area in protest at the introduction of power looms in the mills, bread prices, and the 'Swing Riots' of agricultural workers destroying threshing machines particularly in the Fairford and Beverstone areas. Short of engaging the regular troops or militia, the proposal for a constabulary force for Gloucestershire was sent to the Home Secretary in 1839 and the Act was adopted and approved for the county on 9 December of that year. Recruiting started immediately. Applicants were required to be under forty-five years old, at least five foot seven inches in height, be able to read, write and keep accounts, be fit and of a strong constitution and generally from a similar background of keeping law, such as gamekeepers, bailiffs and innkeepers. A circular issued from the Cheltenham (then the head) office in 1841 stated:

'The Serjeants and Constables are directed to wear their Old Uniforms on Night Duty and wet days under their Great Coats, and as there is but one pair

of Trousers allowed to each man for the present Year, every attention must be paid to spare them as much as possible ... any of the men to be seen with their Hair and Whiskers in a long and disgusting state as worn by several at present, will be most severely punished.'

Always more humorous in retrospect, the frailties of human life are the constant concern of the police force. Mrs Yeoman recounted a couple of instances of those encountered on the beat seventy years ago:

'In the arms of the law':
in 1939 policewomen
helped with the train-loads
of evacuees which arrived
in the Cotswolds as war
broke out.

'One old lady used to embarrass us considerably when she had had a few drinks. She wore bells sewn on elastic round her knees and if she could find a good audience, such as a cinema queue, she would throw her arms around you, claim to be your long-lost friend and then do a kind of Morris dance, much to the amusement of everyone but us young policewomen. One evening, again in Cheltenham, my attention was attracted by a tram driver ringing his bell furiously. I went over to investigate and he said that a male colleague was at the lower High Street with a drunken woman and needed my help. When I got there I had to relieve him as it was the duty of the policewomen to deal with females – he had tied the woman on to a hand cart as the only way of getting her restrained, although certainly not quiet – and I had to push her on the cart to the station, followed by a procession of men, women and children, all thoroughly enjoying the fun of it.'

Inns

Ye weary travelers that pafs by.
With dust and fcorching funbeams dry
Or be he numb'd with fnow & frost,
With having these bleak cotswolds crofst
Step in and quaff my nut brown ale
Bright as rubys mild and ftale.
Twill make your laging trotters dance
As nimble as the funs of france.
Then ye will own ye men of fense.
That neare was better fpent fix pence.

The Bear at Bisley in 1910. The landlord and his wife are carrying buckets, probably on their way to feed the pigs.

The invitation to sample the hospitality at The Plough Inn at Ford, a pretty hamlet which takes its name quite literally from the head waters of the Windrush settling in a dip in the road, is attributed to Shakespeare, more by cherished tradition than proven fact. Certainly the rambling old hostelry was selling ale in Shakespeare's day.

The Cotswolds must have been a pub-crawler's paradise at one time with inns and hostelries, hotels and beer-houses and off-licences and ale-houses at the ratio of one to every hundred inhabitants. In the course of changing social habits, easier travel and drink-drive curtailment, a number have closed, but there is still an adequate array of genuine old English pubs, each with a long and fascinating history within its thick stone walls.

The oldest can date their foundation back to monastic beginnings to give pilgrims overnight accommodation — such as the magnificent George Hotel at Winchcombe with its steps worn into shallows by the tread of centuries. It still retains its pilgrims gallery, and the initials of the penultimate Abbot of Winchcombe are indelibly carved into the doorway. Many inns are built close to a church, for which the authorities derived a considerable income, hence names like The Cross Keys, The Shaven Crown or the Fish Inn. The Cotswold wool trade is well represented in The Lamb, The Fleece, The Woolpack and The Ram.

'Good ale needs no bush' is an old saying, but a green bough hung outside a house was, at one time, the only licence needed to sell ale or cider. The fishermen on the lower Coln waters at Fairford had their

*'I'm looking towards you,'
is a traditional local toast.
'I catches your eye'
is the expected response.*

*The Ragged Cot, near
Avening: 'Cot' once meant
a shelter for sheep on the
wolds — hence the name
the Cotswolds.*

own little wooden hut on the river meadow and the older people recall having time off school to take luncheon baskets and casks of ale from the Bull Hotel and seeing the branch of hawthorn hanging over the ricketty door. It was known locally as the Old Bull and Bush. In the same way, a small cottage by the town bridge was turned into a pub, called the Bull Tap; the beer was literally tapped by a pipe running under the road from The Bull thereby affording the landlord the running of two houses selling ale under one licence. The Bull Tap was originally for the drovers and labourers, The Bull Hotel for the tradesmen and farmers — but they all drank the same beer.

Inn signs became law under Richard III and, if there was a new brew for sale, an ale garland was hung out on a pole to advertise the fact that the services of the local ale taster was needed, a post appointed by the Court Leet — often, as at Winchcombe, the office seemed hereditary! The reign of George II brought about the licensing laws, and selling ale without licence was a criminal offence and one of the most common of the day, despite harsh penalties which ranged from having personal goods confiscated in lieu of a fine to hard labour for two months 'and on discharge to be stripped naked from the middle upwards and whipped until his body be bloody'.

The historical significance of inn signs is fascinating; many have changed over the years for political or parochial reasons. The Castle Arms of Cromwell's day was returned to its stately status as Sudeley Castle after its ignomious spell as an ale-house.

Adam and Eve in Paradise
God sells beer

This is a Painswickian pun only on the strength of the space inserted into the name of the Godsells who were the brewers supplying the Adam and Eve pub in the hamlet of Paradise, an appositely named spot nestled into a curving dip below the main highway.

Formerly called The Plough, the inn's name was changed in keeping with the celestial community it

The Staircase at The Old Ram Inn, Cirencester.

The grand staircase of the
Old Ram Inn, Cirencester.

served at the time when there was an unholy row as one owner renamed it Goodhurst. Another tried Beechwood. All heaven (and earth too) hold dear is as nought compared with the pride of being a Paradisian. Paradise was regained. Sadly, Adam and Eve closed their doors.

Closing a pub, especially if it is the central spot of a village serving its original purpose of general meeting place for all the parish business, is always a loss to the community life; none could have made the headlines and generated as much interest and support as that of The New Inn at Coln St Aldwyns. The villagers won their battle to save the attractive old inn from being developed into a complex of houses and it reopened. Sharing the same hill, vicar and cricket team is the neighbouring village of Quenington where The Earl Grey claims the title of having the smallest bar in Britain at 12 feet 3 inches by 9 feet 6 inches.

Only the sign indicates that the Ragged Cot, near Avening is a pub; it still retains its Cotswold cottage appearance —the name Cot is an old name for cottage and an even older one for a shelter for sheep on the wolds —from which Cotswolds derived its name. The Bible speaks of 'cotting' sheep and the remnants of shepherds' cots found in isolated spots on the wind-swept hills were of dry stone walls, such as surrounds this old inn.

'I'm looking towards you' is an old local toast. 'I catches your eye' is the traditional reply.

The world has been put to rights over many a glass of ale. Before village halls were built in the Thirties, the business of the parish was always conducted in the genial company of the local hostelry: Overseers, churchwardens, merchants and Justices of the Peace decided on alms, rates, railway viability and inquests. At Hawkesbury, the churchwardens were ordered in 1701 not to 'lay out the Parish money in Taverns or Ale-houses, under pretence of meeting there to despatch business'.

Schools

The formal school photograph: Filkins School.

Be I fond of work? Never done much else, I reckons. I finished with schooling at nine years old, and not much I larned thur neither, 'cepting mischief. I'd a-go on a Monday with me penny if I 'adn't spent un — could get a lot for a penny in them days; never went for the rest of the wik. Me dad, 'ee done an' died just afore I were nine, so I worked under ol' Shep Bants; 'ee was getting on a bit so what 'ee couldn't do, I did, an' I got half a crown a wik. Nearly as much as me ol' dad was getting, so me mother dursn't send I back to schooling with that kind o' money coming in to kip us all. 'Er oodn't be 'aving charity, poor but proud wur the oomanfolk in them days. 'Er 'ad sin many a family off to the workhousen, so 'er sed as 'twas better to have a family wi' full stomicks than a boy wi' 'is yud full o' larnin. That's what a-sed, 'er did.

The Second World War had just ended when old Will Flitter recalled his schooldays of some four score years hence. This was prior to the great Education Act of 1870 which founded the cornerstone of elementary education as a public service to all children. Meanwhile only a selected minority qualified for such charity schools as existed, or received the private tutelage enjoyed by generations of privileged classes.

The school the old nonegenarian had attended so erratically was Fairford Free School, later named Farmor's after Elizabeth Farmor, one of the most foresighted of the eighteenth-century benefactors of Gloucestershire. Most endowments paid for simply the teaching of 'poor children' — mainly boys — and teaching was carried out in church porches, old barns, farmhouse kitchens and lowly cottages.

However, Elizabeth Farmor had left specific instructions in her will for the building of a school with a master's house and it opened in 1738 'to teach sixty poor boys to read English well and also to write a good legible hand'.

Infant School sporting sun hats and bonnets.

Maypole dancing at Bisley School.

*The gardening class at
Farmor's School in 1907.*

A classroom scene in stained glass by Henry Payne for St Loes, near Amberley.

In many schools of the period, writing was treated as an extra to the monotonous timetable of reading scriptural and moralistic texts and the recitation of psalms and catechism.

Gloucestershire as a county authority in general, and the Cotswolds in particular, can claim a long history of education. The earliest school can be traced back to 1100, when a grammar school was annexed to Gloucester Abbey. Throughout the Middle Ages a number of grammar schools, song schools, chantry schools and academies were maintained by collegiate churches or abbeys and suffered the fate of their patrons at the Dissolution. At Winchcombe the Almonry choristers' school was sacked with the monastery but, despite the avaricious henchmen of Henry VIII pinching the lands forming the endowment of the school (although not the property of the Abbey) school was resumed in a house opposite the church with a Crown grant and the title of King's School, under the local authority of the town bailiffs.

The grammar school at Chipping Campden was kept by a priest so it probably started as a chantry school. It was founded in the late fifteenth century. Certificates relating to it were 'sufficiently confusing to enable it to escape confiscation!' A whole century earlier, in 1384, Katharine Lady Berkeley founded a little school for two poor scholars and a master at Wotton-under-Edge. Like Farmor's at Fairford, it is one of four in the county which have survived until today from such ancient foundations.

The prosperous wool marketing towns of Tetbury and Northleach added commercial wealth to ecclesiastical coffers to provide schools of some standing: Sir William Romney specified that the market tolls on wool sold at Tetbury should allow thirteen pounds

Timetable from Daglingworth School set in 1916.

TIME TABLE.

Daglingworth C. of E SCHOOL.   *Mixed* Department

N.B.—The Name of the School entered on this Form should be the Official Name given to it by the Board of Education (as on Form 9).

This Time-Table must show a period of Secular Instruction during one School Meeting of not less than Two Hours (inclusive of Recreation, Arts. 43 (b) & 44 (c)) for each scholar in a School other than an Infant School.

MORNING.

Class	9.15 to 9.40	9.40 to 9.50	9.50 to 10.20	10.20 to 10.45 10.45/11	11 to 11.30	11.30 to 12		1.40 to 1.50	1.50 to 2.15	2.15 to 2.40	2.40 to 2.50	2.50 to 3.10	3.10 to 3.30	3.30 to 3.50

MONDAY.
I. Relig. Inst. Singing S. Reading | Arithmetic Reading Writing — Nat. Study History Recitation | Drawing Modelling Writing
II. " " " " " "
III. " Arithmetic S. Reading Writing Reading — Spelling Copy Books Geography
IV.
V.
VI. (Needlework for Girls all the time) for all Classes
VII.

TUESDAY.
I. Relig. Inst. Phys. Exerc. S. Reading | Arithmetic Geography Reading — Nat. Study Oral Lesson Writing Drill Handwork Spelling
II.
III. " Arithmetic S. Reading Writing — Spelling " History English
IV.
V.
VI.
VII. Nat. Study

WEDNESDAY.
I. Relig. Inst. Singing S. Reading | Arithmetic Reading Writing — Nat. Study History Spelling Singing History | Drawing Modelling Writing
II.
III. " Arithmetic S. Reading Writing Reading — Spelling Singing Handwork
IV.
V. (Needlework for Girls all the time) for all Classes
VI.
VII. Nat. Study

THURSDAY.
I. Relig. Inst. Phys. Exerc. S. Reading | Arithmetic Geography Reading — Nat. Study Oral Lesson Writing Drill Drawing Modelling
II.
III. " Arithmetic S. Reading Writing — Spelling " Geography
IV.
V.
VI.
VII.

FRIDAY.
I. Relig. Inst. Singing S. Reading | Arithmetic Reading Writing — Nat. Study Spelling Singing | Drawing Modelling Writing
II.
III. " Arithmetic S. Reading Writing Reading — Spelling Singing Recitation
IV.
V. (Needlework for Girls all the time) for all Classes
VI.
VII.

RECREATION Ten minutes, or more, vir. Art. 44 (c).

AFTERNOON.

1. Physical Ex.; 2. Singing.

ANALYSIS.

"The Time-Table should contain an analysis by the teacher showing the number of hour devoted to each subject, and the time allotted to recreation and physical exercises."

No. of Minutes per Week devoted to each Subject.	I.	II.	III.	IV.	V.	VI.	VII.
Religious Instruction (Art. 6 & 7)	125	125	125	125			
Moral Instruction (Art. 2)							
SECULAR SUBJECTS (Art. 2)							
1. English Language (Art. 2(1))							
(a) Reading	300	300	275	275			
(b) Recitation	25	25	25	25			
(c) Composition	175	175	40	90			
(d) Spelling & Word-Bldg.	50	50	50	50			
(e) Dictation & Transc.	50	50	60	60			
(f) Grammar							
2. Handwriting (Art. 2(2))	60	60	55	85			
3. Arithmetic (Art. 2(3))	125	125	150	150			
(a) Written	80	8					
(b) Mental (2nd, App. 1.)							
4. Drawing (Art. 2(4))	80	80	80	80			
5. (a) Obs'vation Les (Art.2(5))	50	50	50	50			
(b) Nature-Study (Art. 2(5))	50	50					
6. Geography (Art. 2(6))	60	60	50	50			
7. History (Art. 2(7))	50	50	25	25			
8. Music (Art. 2(8))	50	50	50	50			
9. Hygiene (Art. 2(9))							
10. Physical Training (Art.2(9))	70	70	70	70			
11. Organized Games (Art.44(1))	180	180	180	180			
12. Needlework, &c. (Art.2(10))	180	180	180	180			
13. Special Subjects (Art. 34)							
(a) Cookery (Art. 34)							
(b) Laundry Work (Art.34)							
(c) Domestic Subjects (..)							
(d) Dairy-Work (Art. 34)							
(e) Cook'y (B'y.Sch.iii.19(4))							
(f) Handicraft (Boys,Art. 34)							
(g) Gardening (Boys, Art. 34)							
14. Recreation (Art. 44 (c))	125	125	125	125			
15. Modelling	70	70	70	70			
16.							
17.							

Total No. of Minutes ...
= Hours ...

NOTES.

(1) The Registers are marked at 9.10 a.m. and 1.30 p.m., and are FINALLY CLOSED at 9.55 a.m. and 1.40 p.m. respectively.

(2) Criticism Lessons are given

(i.) Approved on behalf of The Local Education Authority (Art. 7 (c)).

Name ....
Official Position ....
Date 191

(OR)

(ii.) Approved on behalf of The Managers "that to the best of their knowledge it [the Time Table] conflicts with no bye-law as to School Attendance, or direction as to Secular Instruction, made or given by the Local Education Authority under the Education Acts, 1870 to 1904" (Art. 7 (c))

Name .... A.L.R.
Official Position *Official Correspondent*
Date *February 25* 1916

George Gough Head Teacher.
February 9th 1916

Approved on behalf of the Board of Education as fulfilling the requirements of Section 7 of the Elementary Education Act, 1870 (Art. 7 (b)).

.... H.M. Inspector of Schools.
22. 2. 1916.

(The "A.L." Series—No. 1, Upper School.)

towards the salary of 'an honest, godly and sufficient' schoolmaster who was to be 'very skilful in Arithmetic, which art teacheth much wit to all sorts of men and traders, but is too little known in our land'.

No doubt well pleased with the lavish adulation and entertainment of the Cotswold nobility and lesser folk during her stay at Sudeley Castle, Elizabeth I, 'of her royal mind and noble inclination, and of her divine and fervent zeal for the advancement of learning and good literature', decreed that the Chantry Commissioners should grant lands from the old chantry at Cheltenham to endow a grammar school. Richard Pate duly built such a school in 1571 in the High Street close by the church.

Up on the wolds at Stow, the grammar school did not attract the attention of 'good Queen Bess' — possibly because it was one of the few places that could lay claim to her *not* having slept there! The school was said to be in a 'ruinous condition' in her time and was rescued by a local merchant tailor who left twelve pounds per annum for 'a discreet, pious and learned man to teach the Latin tongue and other more polite literature and science'.

'You that are rich ought thus to take care of the education of the poor', was the rallying call of the curate, John Jackson at Dursley, appealing to the wealthy clothiers and mill-owners of the district to start a subscription school. '... powerful advocates these poor children will be for you at Christ's Tribunal, how triumphantly will you be usher'd in and with what confidence appear before the Judge'. This could be the reward for educating 'happy little souls, whom you have rescued from the Devil'. The charity school opened in 1710 with the support of the SPCK, but lasted less than a decade.

Promoting Christian knowledge with or without the assistance of the Society lay at the core of the elementary educational system which put down its tenuous roots in the Cotswolds. The Sunday School movement became a national institution of incalculable influence. Whitfield and Wesley had founded schools in Gloucester and Robert Raikes centred his network of Sunday schools in the city too, but it was a Cotswold man who established the system on the countryside in which he had spent his childhood bird-scaring and leading a team at plough.

William Fox was born at the hardly-a-hamlet of Clapton, above Bourton-on-the-Water. From his lowly beginnings he sought and secured a fortune in commerce in London. Returning to his country home, Fox bought the manorial estate and used his influence and wealth to establish a school during the week — as well as a Sunday school — and formulated plans for a Sunday School Society.

Raikes and Fox were both in attendance at the Painswick Sunday School festival in 1786, celebrating the school founded by Edward Webb, a clothier. The order and spectacle of 331 children lined up outside the church, to be inspected by the local gentry and dignitaries, many of whom were 'such keen scholars that they worked at their looms with their books at their side ready to be taken up at the first opportunity', impressed all who surveyed the scene and the sermon to which they dutifully listened afterwards was published in the *Gentleman's Magazine*.

The Stroud Valley, punctuated with the cloth mills upon which the local people expended their youth and energy to eke out a hard living, was a pitch upon which religious politics were constantly played out. The fervour of non-conformity took a deep hold in industrialised areas, while on the wolds — where the living was locked into the land of the manorial estates with their nigh-on medieval ties of tenure — the established church weathered the vagaries of religious fashion.

Christian education is the nucleus of the British educational system, and it is from the religious convictions or persuasions of the promoters that we can trace the 'British' or 'National' foundations of most of the Cotswold schools. British schools were founded mainly from the Sunday School movement of the nonconformist chapels. Centred on the whole in towns and the cloth-making areas, the 'British System for the Education of the Labouring and Manufacturing Classes of Society of Every Religious Persuasion' raised relatively few school buildings in the Cotswolds. Two words shorter in title, but years longer in history, the 'National Society for the Education of the Poor in the Principles of the Established Church' had its roots in the chantry and charity schools closely linked to church and manor. The government of the day, pressed to introduce legislation to educate the populace, made a tentative step towards state aid in 1833 by allocating £20,000 as a national educational budget, to be divided equally between the two denominational societies as a means of supplementing the voluntary subscriptions which had hitherto funded such schools as existed.

It is really only from the time of such state aid that we can glean any insight of early schooling. Again, it was a Cotswold man, Lord John Russell, MP for Stroud, who spearheaded an important step in national education. Promoting the principle of 'superintending the application of any sums voted by Parliament for the purpose of instituting public education', Lord Russell advocated the need for a Committee of the Privy Council — the forerunner of a Ministry of Education.... The day of the dreaded Her Majesty's Inspectorate had dawned.

In 1844 the Reverend H W Bellairs carried out the first of these and reported back some startling evidence of some of the schools in the Cotswolds.

At Winstone, between Cirencester and Gloucester, the school was under the charge of a shepherd who, at the venerable age of eighty, was deemed too old and infirm to tend his sheep, so had undertaken the education of the village children, to whom he taught 'very elementary writing'.

*The shiny-buttoned Blue
Coat uniform of Bisley
School in about 1885.*

*Games in the playground:
skipping and ring games
re-enacting many aspects of
family life have been
passed down from
generation to generation.*

*Eight o'clock is striking: Mother, may I go out?
For my young man is waiting to take me round about
First he bought me apples, then he bought me pears
And then he gave me sixpence to kiss him on the stairs*

Infirmity from rheumatism and old age had directed an 'illiterate labourer' at Stoke Orchard to 'teach school' to the local children.

The parish clerk at Duntisbourne Abbots was worse than useless and 'had no skill for teaching', and at Badgeworth, the schoolmarm was said to 'be almost as strikingly ignorant as the children'.

'It aint much they pays I, and it aint much I larns 'em', said one old woman who ran a dame school, the children huddled into a corner of her tiny tollhouse, sharing one tattered copy of *The Whole Duty of Man* between running out to raise the tollbar for passing carts and carriages.

Just what was learnt, and how it was taught, and how much the school received in the form of the meagre and hard won 'Grant' had to be recorded in a log book of daily entries from 1862. It is from these stoutly bound, lock and clasp diaries 'of not less than 500 ruled pages', that a keyhole into the classrooms of the past was forged. Personal observations were strictly forbidden as illustrated by this entry from a Down Ampney schoolmaster, emboldened to vent his frustration on the eve of his departure following a scathing HMI Report. The master blamed the vicar for not having the windows mended — as Correspondent this was one of the Vicar's responsibilities. He also claimed that he had not provided sufficient slates for the children to work on and that he had been hanging on to the Report. The master's toothache which rampaged mercilessly over six months' entries obviously did not help his frame of mind.

'As the log-book is to contain nothing of a personal nature I refrain from giving my opinion regarding Mr Balmer's fitness for an Inspector, but were I to, he would hardly feel flattered....I shall be glad to leave a district where the Inspector is such a friend to "progress" as to suppose he can examine 50 or so children in their knowledge of Reading, Writing and Arithmetic in 50 minutes ...were I Manager of the school I would demand another examination by another Inspector ...I will willingly draw the curtain and say goodbye to him.'

The master left immediately after, and his successor noted that the key to the log book had gone with him! Veiled innuendoes against bossy vicars, Lords of the Manor and all they surveyed and stood for, My Lords

One of the last of the old school road-signs left in the Cotswolds.

The school clock at Coates commemorates the coronation of George V. A peppercorn rent for hanging the clock, of one shilling a year, was charged from 1911 until the school closed in 1987.

Arms are neatly folded in this rare indoor school class photograph.

With evacuee labels and gasmasks, Cockney children arrive at Chipping Norton, watched by the village bobby.

*A First World War
school certificate.*

of HM Inspectorate and their omniscient power, belligerent parents, recalcitrant pupils and petrified pupil teachers linger between the carefully written lines; spectres of schooldays past, which otherwise read as dull as ditchwater. Such vignettes of village life add some spice to the tedium of a restricted curriculum. HM Inspectorate seem always to find little to praise and much to criticize. Grants were made 'with hesitation' if the singing was a bit off-key or the mistress was reluctant to show her calico work!

Acceptance of the Grant abolished school pence, many a vicar expressed his concern on how the penny saved on state-aided schooling might be frittered away by families unused to having a penny to call their own — so he is to be spied amongst the entries introducing the School Bank. But as the Monday deposits ended up as Thursday withdrawals the system did not last long in most schools. As well as the educational prowess and progress of the pupils, the dreaded Inspection also surveyed fabric, furnishing and equipment; a smoky chimney, cracked flue-pot and a mouse-inhabited harmonium were categorized as 'insufficient', along with monitors who couldn't keep 'the babies' falling off the narrow planks that served as seats in the galleries, and masters whose nervous demeanour made them suspect. Average attendance was the yardstick by which a large portion of the 'available grant' was measured, and the bane of the master's life.

Absences were calculated against 'times open', so many a long-suffering master hastily closed school when the counter attractions of circuses, fairs, feasts and choir outings, Club walks and Sunday School treats, beating for the local shoot, nursing the baby while mother went harvesting, looking after the farmers' pigs, tolling the bell or a 'sale of cheap hats' (as at Fairford once) took his charges from the cramped iron-framed desk to join the outside world for the day.

ELEMENTARY EDUCATION ACT, 1876. Education Department Form No. **146.**

CERTIFICATE OF PROFICIENCY.

I do hereby, in pursuance of authority for that purpose delegated to me under the hand of _J P Balmer Esq_, H.M. Inspector of Schools, certify that _Charles Morse_ residing at _Mt Pleasant_ aged _11_ (last birthday) has reached the _IV_ Standard of Proficiency fixed by the Code of the Education Department.

Signed this _2_ day of _October_ 18_88_

John Taylor

Head Teacher

Office* of person } certifying.

*e.g. Teacher of _____ Public Elementary, or Certified Efficient, School; or Clerk, (or Officer) of the School Board, or School Attendance Committee, or Local Committee of _____ County of _____

The 'Certificate of Proficiency' was awarded to children who passed Standard IV, regardless of age. The eleven-year-old boy, in this case, had reached the standard of education required and could leave school.

PUNISHMENT BOOK.

10

Year 19**37**

Date: Month & Day	Name of Scholar	Std. or Class	Nature of Offence	Punishment	Signature (or Initials) of Teacher who Administered the Punishment
20th April	Haines, Sidney	II B	Deliberate disobedience	4 strokes	FEB
20th "	Day, Leonard	II B	"	4 "	FEB
29th "	Harber, Ronald	II B	"	2 "	FEB
30th "	Habgood, Edith	II A	Deliberate disobedience; playing leap-frog in the playground	4	FEB
30th "	Day, Leonard	II B	"	4	FEB
7th May	Simms, Alfred	II B	Rough behaviour in the playground	4	FEB
3rd June	Garlick, Charles	II A	Persistant disobedience	4	FEB
10th "	Simms, Alfred	II B	Rough behaviour in the playground	6	FEB
13th July	Garlick, Reuben	II B	Persistent disobedience & untruthfulness	6	FEB
29th "	Garlick, Charles	II A	Disobedience	2	FEB
29th "	Haines, Sidney	II B	"	2 "	FEB
29th "	Bownes, Margaret	II A	Deceit	2	FEB
8th Sept.	Haines, Sidney	II A	Persistent disobedience	4	FEB
"	Carpenter, John	II A	"	4	FEB
"	Harber, Ronald	II B	"	2 "	FEB
"	Francis, Denys	II B	"	2 "	FEB
4th Nov.	Haines, Raymond	II B	Throwing berries into school through the window	4	FEB
15th "	Jones, Horace	II B	Repeated disobedience	4 "	FEB
"	Francis, Denys	II B	" "	4 "	FEB

School punishment book from 1937: several children were involved in throwing berries through the school window — quite a feat when the height and inward-tilting angle of the window are taken into account. Six strokes was evidently the maximum punishment, for bringing matches and cigarette ends to school and for trying to smoke moss in a home-made pipe. Disobedience and rough behaviour in the playground are frequent offences and it appears that leapfrog was also banned.

In many schools it was well into the Twenties before boys and girls sat together in class and, even so, in some cases the wall which divided the playgrounds did not disappear until the Swinging Sixties.

Closure of the village schools is never without strong local opposition for they still remain the hub of the community and forge the strongest links between the past, present and future.

Punishments were meted out for the pettiest of crimes in most cases and had to be recorded in the Punishment Book.

1881 13 October Lechlade
Whipped a little boy for telling a lie.

1882 6 January
Caned two little girls for telling a falsehood.

1902
Aldwyn Humphries 4 stripes on 'hind quarters' for laughing during prayers.

1904 13 January Kempsford
Harold Couling refused to hold out his hand for punishment so I gave him 5 stripes on his body.

1921
May Pitchers, smack on forearm for wasting time in Composition.

Meysey Hampton
Kate Prophett and Dorothy Drew one stroke each for giggling.

1922 23 June North Cerney
Punished E Savory by a stroke on each hand for opening the gate between the boys' and girls' playgrounds.

The entire village school clustered on the doorstep for the final few minutes of Daglingworth School on its last day. When the whole school numbers less than a football team, closure is an inevitable but irreparable loss to the community.

The odd skirmish between school master or mistress, parent and pupil is also revealed.

1886 12 November Finstock
Admitted Lizzy Holyfield and William Busby, both over 5 years and not been at school before. They live with their grandparents who take them about the country a great deal. At present they seem absolutely without intelligence. In short they are almost, if not quite, like savages.

1878 1 February Hatherop
Taught the children a new song,
The Huntsman's Chorus.

1878 3 February
Mary Anne, Mirriam and Ruth Godwin withdrawn as their father would not allow them to sing it, saying it was a song inspired by Satan.

1890 Temple Guiting
Mr Bishop objects to his children sweeping the schoolroom, I told him of the rule which has been in force for many years.

1895 11 January Amberley
I was informed that Edward Glastonbury had obtained and caused to be burnt one of the scholar's deposit bank books. I gave him a reprimand and two or three light strokes across the back. On returning to school for the afternoon session I was suddenly and violently assaulted by Mrs Glastonbury—receiving three severe blows (two on the face) from a huge stick and stones which she had in her possession. Her language was of a most foul and threatening character.... she frequently attempted to bite me.

Absentees

Local funerals were all well supported by snivelling children who had no idea for whom they were showing such emotion — theirs was not to question who it was they were mourning; they were only too glad someone had afforded them another excuse to skip school. As Pop Curtis recalled, casting his long memory back to his schooldays at Withington at the turn of the century:

'"Seems very fond of funerals, you do," our old master said to us one day after we joined someone's so as to miss school for the afternoon. "Well, you boys can come to my Nanny's tomorrow!"

We thought our luck was in, to be actually invited: it might even mean we could join in the ham tea as most of the families put on for such occasions.

Next day he had us lined up on the school path, our caps tightly screwed up in our grubby little fists so as we could give our nose a wipe all respectful like at the right time. Then, round from the back comes the old schoolmaster pushing a wheelbarrow and beckoned to us to follow. We shuffled along not knowing what to think —him the master chantering and chuntering away like some old parson, so we joined in the muttering of some hymn or other with our heads down, well we hadn't actually seen a dead person in a wheelbarrow before —they'd all been in coffins, proper like. Then he stopped under the old apple tree at the top of the garden and told us to pick up the shovels propped against it to dig a big hole. Well, we were that frit, I can tell you. I walked on with my eyes screwed up as not to see the body in the barrow, but I bumped into it as I couldn't see where I was going. Then I could see these four legs sticking up in the air. It was his old Nanny goat he was getting us to follow and bury for him.

We never missed school for another funeral, I can tell you.'

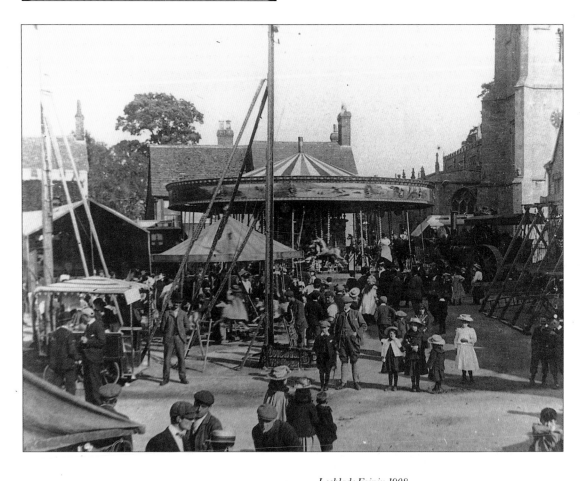

Lechlade Fair in 1908.
Schools often closed when
the children had to help at
the harvest, gleaning or
haymaking — or if there
was strong competition for
their attentions, such as
when the fair arrived
in town.

Awards ranged from medals engraved 'Never Absent, Never Late' on the one side and, on the other, the name of achiever of this (remarkable for the age) feat to certificates and books and, on occasion, a silver watch for full attendance. Bribes in the form of 'the vicar's shilling' were also offered in an attempt to achieve that elusive entry of 'full attendance'. When that failed, and The Inspection was imminent, downright bullying was called for.

'May I remind parents that My Lords will be inspecting the school on Monday next, and I shall expect every child to come to school with clean hands and face, and boots well brushed. Those not in their place at nine o'clock will be spiflicated,' warned the master of Fairford Infant School in 1897.

A random turning of the pages of log books in the Cotswold village schools will create little word pictures of social conditions and changes, of the influence the country pursuits and patriotic loyalties had on the communities the schools served, and how closely knit they were into the life and traditions of their villages.

1871: 21 December Down Ampney
The children gone A-Thomasin. They follow the ancient custom here of going to the farms for pence. Known by the scholars as begging day.

1876: 10 September
Attendance very small. Several fields in village still to be gleaned.

1876: 21 September
Monitor absent — gleaning.

1883: 11 October Coates
Ciren Mop on Monday and Wombold's Menagerie on Friday caused irregularity.

1886: 5 October Hatherop
Nine children died of scarlet fever. Charlie Kibble left early to drive a cow to Quenington.

1887: 25 July Powells
Commenced on Monday with 183, which fell on Friday afternoon to 165, probably from rumours that the Harvest will be much earlier than was expected and that the corn is already cut in some of the neighbouring villages.

1887: 26 September
This being Nutting Week, Monday is granted as the usual holiday as Earl Bathurst has opened Cirencester Park to the public to gather nuts.

1888: 30 July
The usual Address, scrambling for ginger and other nuts, cheering for the teachers, with 'God Save the Queen' — the customary close for Harvest Holiday.

1890: Temple Guiting
The people around here make it a general holiday to go to Winchcombe Volunteer Review. Children absent on their annual treat. Mr. C. Lane took them with his traction engine and two waggons to Farmcote (5 miles) where they spent an enjoyable afternoon and evening.

1905: 25 July Wychwoods
Mothers Club meeting, all choir boys absent in consequence.

1905: 1 August
Many absent owing to the Chapel school treat at Capps Lodge.

1905: 25 September
Burford Hiring Fair — several absent.

1905: 11 October
Chipping Norton Hiring Fair — several absent in consequence.

1908: 13 May North Cerney
Several absent owing to dandelion picking for wine.

1911
Lady Carrington gave mugs, jugs and a saucepan for the Head's wife to make hot cocoa for the pupils at $\frac{1}{2}$d per $\frac{1}{2}$ pint cup — thus making a profit of 1d a day for the school.

1934: 8 January Guiting Power
School closed in the afternoon as the Point to Point Races are again at Roel Gate and the majority of parents attend with their children.

HOME LIFE AND HOLIDAYS

From cradle
to grave

'The Cotswold people are, like their country, healthy, bright, clean, and old-fashioned ... they are not half-educated and half-refined, but simple, honest, god-fearing folk, who mind their own business and have not sought out many inventions. A primitive people, as often as not they are "nature's gentlemen".'
J Arthur Gibbs

W hile it is true that Cotswold folk do mind their own business, it was the way of life in the days when cottages were small and families large that life tumbled out into the lanes and gardens and the village streets. Such was the interdependence and integration of each with the other that one family's business was bound up with the concern of others. And life itself was the warp across which superstition and tradition were the weft so that the fabric of distinct culture was woven from many sources and origins.

The alpha and omega were simply birth and death. Each had its attendant niceties and customs to observe — a curious admix of pagan beliefs and biblical parables and Shakespearian sagacity.

The owl shriek'd at thy birth, an evil sign!
The night crow cry'd, aboding luckless time;
Dogs howl'd and hideous tempests shook down trees

With such a cacophonous fanfare from bird and beast, Richard III, Duke of Gloucester and later King of England, was obviously a marked man at birth.

It was also ill-fated to be born on a Good Friday:
Who is born on that night will never see sprite.

It was even worse if the parents turned elder wood into a cradle, for its long association with witchcraft meant that the expected child would not live long enough to see night, let alone sprite.

Even if the child survived the coming into this world there were still precautions to take to prepare him or her for the next. Christenings often took place in the bedroom, the rose-patterned hand basin on the washstand being suitably blessed as an interim measure should the child's health give rise for concern. Unchristened children were subject to all kinds of danger from witches and wicked fairies, so spells had to be diffused before they could be cast. The Cotswold trinity was a pair of open scissors hung over

Photograph on page 72
Bledington Band of Hope annual outing in a harvest wagon to Sarsden Lodge. The temperance band would play, there was tea from a portable boiler and the farmer's wife made dolls as prizes for the girls' three-legged race.

Photograph on page 73
Fifteen-year-old Delaretha looks after baby Mabel who is aged ten months and sits in an ornate perambulator.

Henry at ten months old: baby boys were just as frilled, beribboned and bonneted as were their little sisters.

The receipts at Ebrington Church show a charge of sixpence for the 'churching' of a newly-delivered mother, as well as varying charges for weddings and funerals.

Family group in the back yard in about 1890.

the cradle, the pins in the baby's clothing must be crossed and father had to lay his unfolded trousers across the cradle.

Churching of the mother, as a thanksgiving for a safe confinement, and to give a church blessing on the child, was strictly an Anglican custom. It had to be done before the mother went out with the child, so a special and simple little service was carried out with only the vicar and mother involved, and that was her first outing. According to Ebrington Church Receipts, it cost sixpence for Churching in 1821.

The bustle of the local midwife and neighbours pumping water into buckets to fill the pans on the fire and the rest of the family scurrying around gave its own warning to the community that 'the house is on fire', as they said of a birth. When all was safely delivered, father would be hailed as some kind of hero at the local pub, pressed with drinks 'to wet the baby's head'. And the question would be whether it was 'boy or child'! One oft-quoted tale is that of a man who on being asked, 'Well, Jarge, was it a boy!', replied by a shake of his head. 'Ah, then,' his neighbour concluded — with the smile of assurance that his intelligence in these matters singled him out as being quite quick-witted — 'it must be a girl'. The father, who had enjoyed being the centre of such attraction, was quite deflated and agreed, in a bit of pique: 'then someone must have told thee'.

The next step was the christening. At Ascott-under-Wychwood, which was formerly known as East Cote, the blocked-up Norman doorway of the church was said to be where the devil made his exit whenever he lost a little soul to the church.

While the popular concept of Victorian life is that of large families doted upon by god-fearing parents, the harsh reality of numerous hungry little mouths to feed and backs to clothe was a constant worry. There was a belief that a woman would not conceive again while breast-feeding her baby, and many a toddler continued suckling on the strength of it. 'Wet-nurses' were employed by the well-to-do whose social commitments and pleasures left them no time or inclination for such lowly responsibilities. Local recently-confined mothers were therefore entrusted with sharing their natural milk between their own newly-born and that of the new manorial heir.

Only the well-off or carpenter-clever had cradles, apart from family heirlooms which were a matter of great pride; others had to make do with wicker baskets, often a large clothes basket, lined with blankets, or, more usually, and well within living memory, a drawer out of a chest of drawers. The amount of 'swaddling' swaddled round the little mite must have been suffocating. Belly-bands bound round the middle, with a penny piece laid flat on the navel to stop it protruding, flannel and cambric and calico in layers of bodices and petticoats and back flannels and gowns and bonnets kept the child well and truly in a tidy bundle. Little boys were 'frocked' until the age of three—when they were sent off to school if the parents were keen on education.

On the whole, clothes were handmade and exquisite in their tiny-stitched detail of frills and flounces and eyelet holes. As a child got older, it was very much a case of cut-down hand-me-downs and therefore the pictures we see of our grandparents are of little people in grown-up clothes tucked in and chopped off.

Family cure-alls

The village venerable Mrs Gamp, whose presence was essential at the bringing unto this world and the laying out for the next, was the matriach mentor for all the frailties and failings of the body between its Genesis and Exodus. She operated under the badge of honourable experience of life such as Widow or Granny and the community was largely at her mercy and magic, for it was she who knew the cures 'for all the complaints no-one ever dies of'.

For those who could not afford the pills and potions, unctions and lotions advertised so prolifically in the newspapers, the garden and hedgerow were their dispensary. Gatherings, ulcers, boils and other swellings were treated by a poultice of mallow or chickweed. A small onion, heated in the oven, was pressed into an aching ear to give relief (and actually does!); others preferred to make a poultice of poppy petals and bind it round the offending ear. An onion or potato carried in the pocket warded off the 'screwmaticks'. In the north Cotswolds the remedy for rheumatic twinges was a wineglassful of an infusion of traveller's joy leaves. Daglingworth believed more in bee stings and Grampy Wallington of Lechlade used to beat himself vigorously with stinging nettles. At Stanton they turned to the church; confirmation was believed to rid one of the dreaded pain and one servant at Stanton Court is reported to have been confirmed three times in an attempt to be cured.

A Victorian receipt book explains how to make Castor Oil Pomade, an embrocation for whooping cough and Eno's Fruit Salts.

A variety of efficacious tonics and potions from the nineteenth century.

Epilepsy and lunacy, which meant practically the same thing to our ancestors in the not so long ago when every family had someone who 'had fits', were charmed away by wearing necklaces of peony seeds. The roots were strung up and garlanded round the neck of the baby suffering with teething problems.

A sore throat was comforted by wrapping a sock (which was worn but not washed) around the neck and then covering this dubious article with a silk scarf. Toothache had a range of remedies according to the age and sex of the victim. Sturdy stomached grandfathers swore on biting a plug of 'twist baccy'; weaker sons might have a smouldering spill of brown paper held to their nostrils, while delicate daughters bit gently on to a clove if they couldn't afford a small bottle of oil of cloves.

Every family had its favoured cure-all; the Keble family advocated Toast Water for indigestion in the mid-1880s.

Pour boiled water over a slice of blackened toast, leave to steep for two hours, then strain and flavour with a sliver of lemon or orange peel.

In the Dietary of the Dursley Workhouse the Committee recorded that in 1839 the Matron was in the habit of giving bread every night to the paupers to make crust water to drink with their supper, in addition to the one pound bread of their daily ration. It was ordered that it should be allowed.

Hester Keble wrote in her notebook:

Receipt for an asthma
My good old friend, accept from me
the following rules without a fee
An Asthma is your case I think,
so you must neither eat nor drink

I mean of meat preserv'd in salt,
or any liquor made of malt
From season'd sauce avert your eyes
from ham and tongue and pidgeon pyes

If venison patty is sett before you,
each bitt you eat Memento Mori
Your supper, nothing if you please,
but above all no toasted cheese
Tis likely you will now observe
that I prescribe will make you starve
No — I allow you at a meal
a leg, a loyn, or neck of veal
Young turkeys I allow you four,
partridge or pullets half a score
Of house lamb boyld, eat quarters two,
the devil's in it if that won't doe

Now as to liquor, why indeed,
what I advise — I send you mead
Glass's of this to extinquish the drought,
take three with water, three wi'out
Lett constant exercise by tryed
and sometimes walk, sometimes ride
Health oftener comes from Blackdown Hill
than from the apothecary's pill

For breakfast it is my advice
eat gruel, sago, barley, rice
Take burdock roots and by my troth,
I'd mingle daisies in my broth
Thus may you draw with ease your breath,
eluding long the dart of death
Thus may you laugh; look clear and thrive,
enrich'd by those whom you survive

Miriam Jane Pedley's Cure for a Cold (1868)
Put 1 lb Turkey figs, each cut into 8 parts, with 1 lb sugar candy, finely powdered, and the juice of one lemon with $\frac{1}{2}$ pint of rum. Let it stand for 24 hours, then take a little occasionally until the head clears.

Aunt Bessie's Blood Purifier
Gather the tops of young nettles, wash well under water pumped straight over them. To every pound of nettles add a quart of freshly drawn water. Put into a pot over the fire and boil for one hour. Strain and to every pint of juice add a pound of sugar, then boil for another 30 minutes. Bottle when cold.

Clergymen's wives were renowned for their fund of tried and true tonics and potions. Whole villages got cured of all kinds of cuts and bumps around the Rissingtons from:

Nora Cheale's Aunt Mary's Ointment.
2 ozs beeswax, cut up small
2 ozs white powdered resin
2 ozs butter straight from the churn
Mix all together over a slow fire and pour into china pots.

More serious complaints demanded stronger measures. Gretton children who were suffering from whooping cough were ordered a pulling through the arch made by a briar rooted at both ends first thing in the morning for three days in succession. The churchwarden declared the method 'a cruel remedy' in 1891 and 'was glad to hear it was dying out'. Other chest-complainted youngsters were trundled up the road to where repairs were being carried out and hung over the vaporizing tar fumes 'to assist their breathing'. Ricketty children were passed through the large holes in the monoliths scattered around the Stroud valley; the Tingle stone was accredited with powers 'beyond belief'. Weak eyes were strengthened by bathing in weak tea throughout the year and magically so on May Day when the countryfolk bathed in the dew and collected the spring water on Palm Sunday in Wychwood Forest — a custom still carried out. A 'stye' on the eyelid was made better by rubbing a wedding ring along the 'teart' spot.

The only effective relief for agonizing chilblains, families swore by, was for the painful foot to be dipped in the chamber pot — of the sufferer's own using! Nothing was wasted, not even the slops. Granny Morse had the best roses in Mount Pleasant from using her slops on the bushes by the front door, once, that is, old Eustace Crook had given up his round, collecting them in a big drum in the back of a donkey cart for use in his tanyard.

Prevention being the proverbial better than cure, great lengths were taken to keep the family fit. Home-brewed wines and hot toddies, blackcurrant tea, thick onion soup, port wine and quinine — as well as inherited receipts for blood purifiers and tonics were the general standbys.

The most drastic measure though, which Pop Morse related as having been carried out on children in the 1880s was being wrapped up for winter. Goose-grease was spread thickly on the child's chest and back in the autumn, wrapped round with several layers of thick brown paper, then a flannel vest was literally stitched on 'as far as possible' and left until spring peeped over the Cotswold hills.

Thorns and corns

A Winchcombe cure was said to have been witnessed at the end of the last century of a local old wise woman making a circle round an inbedded thorn in the finger and chanting:

> *In Bethlehem one Christ was born*
> *And crowned with a crown of thorns*
> *It never festered, never swelled*
> *I hope to Christ it never will.*

Corns were removed with less drama: an ivy leaf soaked in vinegar and bound round the toe above the corn, repeated for three successive days; the juice of red campion squeezed direct on the corn; or the juice of the greater celandine. These cures preceded all the pads and proprietary potions available today — and were said to have worked.

Boneshave

One of my favourite fables from the family store is that of my Granny having resorted to seek the doctor's diagnosis of a painful knee. On being told it was just old age, Granny snorted 'Well doctor, it can't be that; the other knee is alright and they're both the same age'.

It may be that she had not found a stream conveniently running south, an important element in the cure for boneshave (sciatica). Had she found one she should have recited this little ditty thrice, while lying on the ground:

> *Boneshave right, boneshave straight*
> *As the water runs by the stave*
> *So follows boneshave.*

[The stave meant a bush or a tree.]

A late-Victorian wedding group clustered on kitchen chairs in a back courtyard.

A-courting they did go

Last Friday was Valentine's Day, and the night before I got five bay leaves and pinned four of them to the four corners of my pillow, and the fifth in the middle; and then if I dreamt of my sweetheart, Betty said, we should be married before the year was out. But to make it more sure, I boiled an egg hard, and took out the yoke [yolk] and filled it with salt, and when I went to bed, ate it shell and all without speaking, or drinking after it. We also wrote our lovers' names on bits of paper, and rolled them up in clay, and put them in water, and the first that rose up was to be our Valentine. Would you believe it? Mr Blossom was my man. I lay a-bed, and shut my eyes all the morning, till he came to our house; for I would not have seen another man before him for all the world.

This young maid's account from the north Cotswolds in 1754 combines the ancient folk spell element with an even older form of lottery, which was practised by the Romans, in a home-spun attempt at telling one's love fortunes.

The rituals of seeking a passionate path to the altar vary from region to region. In the far south Cotswolds a two- or four-leafed clover was placed in the right shoe and the next man to cross the lady's path would be her future love. In the Hailes countryside it was more a chance of dreams to identify the unsuspecting intended, but not without the proper course of action to prompt them. Pinning her garters to the wall, and laying her shoes down in the shape of a T, the next step was to approach the bed backwards and chant:

I pin my garters to the wall
And leave my shoes in the shape of a T
In the trust my true love appears to me
Not in riches, nor in fine array
But in clothes he do wear any old day

Childhood sweethearts
in about 1900.

Lad's Love, appropriately named, was the plant to be worn in the shoe in the north-west Cotswolds to come upon your lover by chance. Lovers' Candles were ordinary white household candles carried upstairs to light lovelorn lassies to bed perchance to dream of their sweetheart, providing they had crossed two pins through the candle to pierce the wick. Rather like the 'bidding by a candle' carried out in the area for auctioning small plots of grazing land, the magic worked by the time the flame had reached the crossed pins — and, of course, it had to be helped along with the right incantation:

It's not thee, candle, I aim to pierce
But of my love I wish to hear
So whether he sleeps, or whether awake
I wish my love to me should spake

Even more dramatic, but confined to Christmas, was the making of Dumb Cakes. On Christmas Eve the unmarried girl of the household would make a cake in absolute silence after the rest of the family had retired. Her initials would then be scratched on the top and she would leave it to bake on the top of the dying embers of the fire. Making sure she left the door open she went to bed, in the hope that at midnight her lover would enter and cut his initials in the top of the cake by the side of hers. In the morning (if the cake wasn't by then a cinder) the young lady would accept this silent proposal by eating the cake — this action again carried out in total silence.

After all these attractive overtures had achieved their desired response, the couple would be seen 'walking out'. Courting was carried on out of doors because an extra mouth to feed would have been beyond the table of the poorer families. However, once things became serious then the sweetheart was duly taken home for Sunday tea — there to be appraised by the rest of the family.

When they were married

'Mistaken souls who dream of heaven ...' Amen

Thus pronounced the loud *sotto voce* of the old clerk after a vicar had called the banns of an 'intended' couple. In another parish, when the priest asked, 'Who giveth this woman...?', the father replied, 'Well, sir, I be called to be doing on't. But I does it agin the grain. I wanted 'er to marry Bill Plowser — he's wuth twice the money o' that ere man.'

Love in a Cottage — nonsense! Among the *Pickings from Punch, Extracts from Fun* and *Disraeli's Address, Sputterings from Judy's Pen* sputtered forth the explosion of a marital myth in a local paper in 1873, qualifying her statement by the fact that she had been married for all of six months. 'There is more love in a full flour-barrel than in all the roses and posies and woodbines that ever grew.'

That did not deter the community from enjoying someone else's wedding, especially if it was the son and heir of the Big House — that was always good for a free tea and dancing on the green. The preparations were made well in advance for the wedding of Percy Raymond Barker of Fairford Park in 1874. The *Wilts and Gloucestershire Standard* reported the initial meeting of a handful of worthy tradesmen to discuss the form for local participation 'and right well did these gentlemen devote themselves to the arduous task and handbills were posted to announce tea for all children of the town, as the readiest way of securing co-operation of parents'.

In the fulfilment of time the happy event was stated to have been solemnized with all business in the town suspended. To the peals of the bells and the rousing music of the RNG Militia Band, some four hundred children and their teachers marched to the mansion, to be graciously acknowledged by the squire and the happy couple, whom they in turn cheered 'most lustily' before repairing to a spacious tent 'to amply appease their appetites with a plentiful repast'. A 'course' was staked out and a row of wagons formed a grandstand for the ensuing sports of cricket and quoits, donkey races and an Aunt Sally, with a 'Single v Married' cricket match on the periphery. Bobbing for treacle buns and climbing a greasy pole with the leg of mutton perched on the top as the prize, were followed by dancing. The usual thing was for the servants of the house to dance on the terrace to the reflected gaiety and light-stepping music from the open windows.

The whole village turned out to welcome home to Hatherop Castle the squire, Mr Gardner Bazley, and his bride in 1902. At the end of the road the arch can just be seen. Spanning the road it bore the message: Long Life and Happiness, Welcome Home.

*An Edwardian wedding
group arranged on
the lawn.*

It was obviously an event to be savoured and celebrated for as long as possible, and a couple of weeks later the young bloods of the town made their way down to the railway station to meet the returning honeymooners. To the bewilderment and consternation of the old coachman, the young men took the horses from the carriage and harnessed themselves to draw the young couple the mile and a bit back to the mansion. There they received a 'handsome donation', for which they 'lustily cheered' and cheered themselves even more by repairing to The Bull.

In direct contrast, Baker Shurmer set out for usual on his wedding day with his wickerwork handcart but 'with his Sunday suit and his ears pinned further back', as they say, delivering bread until his half hunter in his best weskit pointed to the appointed hour. Parking his cart outside the church gates, he arrived in church on time and took his beloved as his wife, walked down the church path arm in arm, then left her to go home and prepare whatever there was for the wedding breakfast, while he continued with his bread round.

'Oh, 'twas a long time ago,' one old man reminisces, 'I know I couldn't wait for my young missus to get her stockings off — now I can wait while 'er knits a pair'.

Age-worn maxims, some old sage's saw and good-hearted buffoonery were scattered around like confetti at a wedding: 'Ah, you ties a knot with your tongue, you can't untie with your teeth' is said of taking the vows.

Marry in Lent, you'll be sure to repent.

Marry in haste, repent at leisure.

*Change your name and not the letter,
marry for worse and not for better.*

*When a bachelor puts his hat on his head, his house is
thatched.*

*Love and gunpowder are much the same: one draws you
for miles, the other blows you for miles.*

So many omens and tokens were once observed on the way to the altar it is a wonder our forebears ever got there. Even so, if all the fates were propitious and all customs duly observed, human frailties often upset the happy marriage cart and again became a matter of public concern.

The heinous sin of adultery was given a real trouncing, with wife-beating and hen-pecking a husband almost equally odious ways of breaking up a marriage — seen as contravening church laws.

The Cotswolds practised the rough music and drumming out and riding skimmetty of Hardy's Wessex into living memory. Unpopular neighbours would be literally 'drummed out' of their house to the din of beaten pots and pans and shrills of tin whistles and teeth-gritting rasping on a saw. Scolds were belted into a ducking stool at Winchcombe and dipped into the brook. Harold Greening of Winchcombe recalls a skimmetty ride taking place in his youth, at an hour when all the children were deemed to be abed as this was grown-up doings.

The self-appointed judge and jury of the townsfolk would assemble outside the house of the party or parties who they felt were misdemeaning the bounds of moral decency, and there to the derisive jeers and clatter of pot, pan and fife would haul out one or both offenders. Strapped to a chair or bedstead on top of a cart the defaulting couple were drawn round the town or village accompanied with as much noise and rough music making as could be mustered, contempt and contumely heaped upon them from all sides. The couple would then be dumped back at the house, body and dignity much bruised and dented. If the offending parties could not be brought to boot in person, an effigy of straw, clad in rags, sufficed for the unceremonious ceremony but denied the community the satisfaction of humiliating the offenders directly.

Gone but not forgotten

Betty dear, my love,
You've turned to grass;
I've travelled along the road and I'm weary,
Now I'll pay my best regards, old deary.

The message tied to a jam-jar of bright yellow daffodils appeared one morning on Betty's Grave. But two hundred Springs had passed from the time Betty was laid to rest at the crossroads between Cirencester and Quenington and the anonymous payer of the respects. Betty's Grave has seldom been without flowers though, and no-one has ever seen them placed there. Folk say it is the gypsies passing that way — but the last of the true deddicoys pass by less frequently nowadays, and us locals 'know someone who knows' where the flowers come from. But who was Betty and why is she buried on the lonely country crossroads? That she lived and died is certain — but how many times — is not. The legend has probably eclipsed the fact. The belief that she was a witch, a poisoner, a sheep-stealer or died at that spot from exhaustion after proving a wager that she could cut a field of hay in a day single-handed, can be neither proved nor discounted. What cannot be disputed is the fact that a certain Elizabeth

Betty's grave

Bastoe of Poulton lives on in folk-tales and is accorded the distinction of being on the Ordnance Survey map and a postal spot.

Romantic tragedies have been the poet's inspiration throughout the ages, and Thomas Haynes Bayly made the sad story of the bride of Minster Lovell Hall, hiding in an oak chest on her wedding night festivities, into the haunting and most enduring poem as *The Mistletoe Bough*. The gaunt ruins of the once stately Hall on the banks of the Windrush stand sentinel as a melancholic memorial to its past.

The quaint but quite ineffectual Burial in Woollen Act was not so much in consideration for the deceased as an attempt to maintain the place wool had in the then declining economy.

This certificate with its merry mix of crude and cosy illustration is dated 1684. It certifies that Richard George of Bagendon swore an affidavit that the departed Richard 'was not put in, wrapt, or wound up or buried, in any shirt, shift, sheet or shroud made or mingled with flax, hemp, silk, hair, gold or silver or other than what is made of sheeps wool only, nor in any coffin lined or faced with any cloth, stuff or any other thing whatsoever but sheeps wool.' Introduced at the Restoration to stimulate the wool trade which had suffered along with everything else during the Civil War, the fine for evading the law was five pounds, shared between the informant and the poor of the parish. Imposing the regulations proved more difficult and the Act was finally repealed in 1800.

Accepting that death is part of life, the passing of a neighbour was, if not a community affair, at least of direct concern to the immediate next-doors. In the days before chapels of rest, keeping the body at home was beset with problems and a steady stream of respect payers traipsed to and through the small cottages to gaze upon the departed. 'Ah, Missus,' one old soul was comforting the bereaved, 'Your Amos is looking that peaceful he'll be with the angels tonight

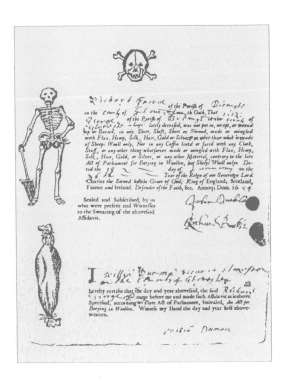

Certificate from 1684 following the Burial in Woollen Act.

Leighterton churchyard: graves of airmen from the nearby air-training field (mainly Australians and New Zealanders) who lost their lives during the First World War. An Anzac Day is still held annually.

Minster Lovell, where a romantic tragedy occurred when a bride hid in an oak chest during a game of hide and seek at the wedding festivities. She was unable to raise the lid again and, as no-one could find her, she perished there. Her body was not discovered until long afterwards.

third, cutting down an elder tree — half-forgotten omens came out for an airing.

The old people's concern for being 'put away tidy' was well prepared for. Daughters would be versed as to which drawer in the chest held the best nightdress, long white stockings and a white bandage 'I don't want to be going off wi' me mouth all agawp'. Husbands seemed to be resigned to the fact that they would go first and their wives were entrusted to 'see that me doings are done up decent like in a 'handkuchef'. Fear of the humility of a Parish funeral was very real, and scrapings from an already meagre income would be accrued and kept in a secret place 'to see us home'. The pride of the Cotswold family was 'to be buried on ham'. The inevitable 'coming back to the house' was an occasion by which the relatives and neighbours judged the departed and the family would go to any means to make sure that the tea included a goodly joint of home-cured ham.

A set period of mourning was strictly adhered to. Widows wore their weeds for at least six months — often for the remainder of their own lifetime, and many Victorian portraits show the fine black veil over the hair and dresses trimmed with black silk fringe of the widow's weeds. It does not seem that long ago that men wore a band of black satin on their coat sleeve and women a black diamond of satin stitched to their sleeve to show they were in mourning.

Ebrington Church Receipt book shows several entries of 'For a Funeral a black twilled silk hat band and black beaver gloves'.

It is still tradition with some farmers of the Cotswolds to make their last journey in a farm wagon — as shown opposite at the funeral of James Blackwell, farmer and threshing contractor of Farmington.

This is the manner by which William Morris left his home at Kelmscot Manor to be buried in the village churchyard. A simple stone bears only his name, marking the grave.

playing his harp?' Mrs-turned-Widow, hardened by the tough life of the times, pursed her thin lips and replied, 'Now then Annie, don't thee get so mawkish. Fayther'll be doing no such thing, he couldn't manage a tin whistle down yere.'

Recounting the portends before the end kept everyone busy and old wives' tales alive; a clothes line breaking, a robin entering the house, giving roots of lilies or parsley, bringing snowdrops or white lilac into the house, not clearing Christmas greenery away by Twelfth Night; 'green Christmas — full churchyard', or someone having died with their eyes open 'looking for the next', two deaths meaning there must follow a

Funeral of
James Blackwell
of Farmington.

A way of life

The introduction of the small kitchen range was a big step forward for cottagers, who had previously existed on pot-boiled food. A hunk of home-bred bacon went in the bottom of a huge cast-iron cauldron, potatoes and vegetables in season on top. 'I likes my greens to have stars on'm', said old Carter Jefferies, meaning that he enjoyed his cabbage with speckles of fat on it from boiling with the bacon.

Gloucestershire bag puddings embraced all dough-like mixtures boiled in a bag or cloth added to the pot when it reached boiling point. The pot was suspended by a handle hooked on an iron ratchet in the chimney over the open fire. Baked food, like the Sunday joint, when such a rare treat was afforded, was cooked by the local baker once the oven had been cleared of Saturday's bread baking. An advertisement in the *Wilts and Gloucestershire Standard* for 1879 for an oven and stove grate gives the price of 14/9d — available only at The Little Dustpan, Cirencester.

The mantlepiece served as a shelf for the tea caddy, tobacco box, spillholder and salt pot. If a flake of soot hung on the fire bars it foretold a stranger would visit. The way the fire burned was the cottager's weather forecast: bright and sparkling warned of frost, dull and smoky meant rain and if the wind 'whiffled' in the chimney it signalled stormy conditions on the way.

The Romans introduced rabbits to this country, along with 'hoddidimods' — outsize edible snails which thrive in dry stone walls; schoolchildren could earn a shilling a bucketful collected for the pubs whose customers liked them — and the stinging nettle (said to have been imported to warm up the British!). The

Jack Tovey of Eastleach bringing home the bunnies on his bike.

An old privy by Toadsmoor Lake — in use until 1988.

occupation of the Latin legions lives on in many town, road and farm names; Coneygres comes from coney, the name for rabbit used by Shakespeare. Rabbiting was the countryman's means of pest control whilst catching a good wholesome dinner and during the last war it was generally acknowledged that it was rabbit stew which was the family's salvation. Professional rabbiters had to abide by the Rabbit Laws that were passed to ensure rabbits didn't suffer; the Gough family at South Cerney were professional trappers and Isaac Gough delivered an eloquent lobby speech on the subject when a new Rabbit Law was put to the House of Lords at the outbreak of war. Rabbit Clubs were formed in the villages as part of the food production drive, and the rabbit hutch made out of packing cases, old window frames and much ingenuity became a feature in many back yards. The rabbit skins were worth sixpence from the rag and bone man.

'Poor Bisley' Crook, described in the Agricultural Distress Inquiry in 1880 as an eccentric character, was said to have grown forty-seven bushels of wheat per acre for several years in succession:

'Thirty-seven bushels of barley I had this year, and ten bushels the birds took ... done well by a quarter of an acre of cabbages, but little profit from the few pigs.'

Poor Bisley said his two meals a day comprised half a loaf of bread at 6 am, and a 'suetty dump' at 6 pm.

Dump is the Cotswold word for a boiled pudding: dunch dumps are plain; feggy dumps are rich and fruity like a Christmas pudding, and a duff is a dump baked! The Victorians claim to have invented the 'bolster pudding', but John Taylor, the Gloucestershire-born poet wrote in Tudor times of 'the bag-puddings of Gloucestershire' consumed by history's famous glutton, Nicholas Wood.

> *Nympsfield's such a pretty place*
> *Set upon a tump*
> *But all the people eat there*
> *Is ag-pag dump*

So goes a derisive ditty — often penned by rival neighbouring villages. Ag-pag means hedgerow fruit and could be heg-pegs (haws) or wild plums like bulloces.

> *Glo'shire has such vunny places*
> *As anyone yere well knows*
> *Wi' its Uley moggies or Coaley dumps*
> *Cam wi' its yeows and crows*
> *And they do say Dursley baboons*
> *Do yut thur pap*
> *Wi'out any spoons*

'Pap' was a kind of gruel type porridge.

Life in the square at Bibury

Simple household tasks, relaxation and communing with the neighbours all took place outdoors in the summertime

A low garden wall, as here at Bibury, was welcome in the summer months for washing up, cleaning shoes or just enjoying the gramophone — like John Purnell [above], a baker in Arlington, Bibury, in about 1891.

An organ grinder with his ancient breast organ, seen around the Winchcombe-Tewkesbury area about 1890.

The last Knight of the Roads around Coln, Hatherop and Quenington, Charles John finally settled in a shepherd's hut after a lifetime of tramping the Cotswolds.

Gypsy horse and caravan in a country lane.

Village visitors

The isolated life of Cotswold villages was enlivened by a round of itinerant travellers, each plying a unique trade in his or her own season. Faringdon Jack with his hoarse call for 'any old rags, any old bones' drew the cottagers out like Pied Piper. From his throne on top of a heap of obnoxious looking bundles, he would peer down from his perch to produce shiny sixpences for rabbit skins, pared bare bones and a last-resort coat, then click his teeth and the bony brown horse would heave forward against the shafts and pull the cart on to the next street, out of the village and out of sight — presumably back to Faringdon.

Some travelling tradesfolk were known only by the name of the place from whence they hailed: Burford Bill, with his bulbous red nose and great black coat with its capacious inside pockets, could produce all kinds of poached goodies from them and the mysterious bundles on his bicycle handlebars. Shunny Onion appeared like a fieldfare — strings of gold-brown onions weighting down his old bike like coral necklaces. He wore a black beret and was said to be French, so no-one risked getting their tongue round any 'furrin-sounding' name.

With the swallows came Fly-o-Gert, her battered brown cardboard suitcase bursting the stitches along the edges so that tempting glimpses of the contents could be spied. Once inside the house she would open the case with the spotted striped lining and produce 'just the dress for your Annie, off to service I hears' like a conjuror with his rabbit. 'Knows where it comes from, good family', she would coax, holding the said dress against said Annie, stretching or gathering with her scrawny hands to indicate what a good fit it was, with her eye on the fluted china vase on the mantle-piece — 'how much would you be wanting for that old crock?' Bargains struck, case packed with the heir-loom tucked between the boas and bloomers, Fly-o-

Gert flew off on her creaking sit-up-and-beg bike to reappear the following spring.

Bangham Barrett, Chequers and Tiddley Saunders, Bottle Strange and Gallon Baxter, KaKa Wane and Dickie Watts, Holy Joe and Innocent Kate, Paraffin Moses, Gypsy George and Johnny-in-the-Morning — tramps and pedlars and knife-grinders, drovers and dealers, gypsies and tramps, poachers and bible-punchers, wove their colourful thread through the Cotswold once-upon-a-time.

The Knights of the Road, as the tramping fraternity were respectfully dubbed, were to be seen in the same thick almost floor-length coat in summer as well as winter: 'what keeps the cold off, keeps the heat off' was their motto. A tin billycan swinging at the rope that served as a belt would be unhitched and taken to likely looking cottages for hot water. Kind folk obliged with a screw of tea and a hunk of bread and cheese — often in return for a bit of wood chopping.

The secret sign language left by the caller on the gatepost or wall would indicate to any succeeding tramp that it was a good place to beg from. Gypsies were half-feared on account of their supernatural powers, and it was a brave woman who turned the shrewd-eyed, walnut wrinkled gypsy away without buying some trinket or clothes pegs from her great wicker basket.

Forest-fringed Cotswolds held the Wychwood witches — old crones who actually lived in dug-out caves in the wooded dells: Granny Green was one of the last to be remembered, telling fortunes and hawking bits and pieces round the villages and acting as guardian of what was known as the Old Woman's Well set between Shipton-under-Wychwood and Chipping Norton.

Shipton had its 'Mother' prophetess, perhaps not so renowned as her Yorkshire counterpart, but uncannily accurate in her foretelling of a series of disasters in 1893 affecting large numbers of farm animals

Johnny-in-the-Morning was the name given to this pedlar from the Tetbury area. In 1871 a new law was passed on pedlars, whereby the police granted a certificate but held the right to open and examine the pedlar's pack.

throughout the eastern side of the Cotswolds. 'Strange occurances' at The Three Magpies smallholding on the Lechlade to Cirencester road were attributed to the curse of gypsies on their way to market; others blamed Betty, wielding her powers from her grave at the cross-country crossroads. But the cow, owned by Mr Sparrow of The Magpies, thought to have been rendered dry on the strength of Betty's enduring influence, turned out to have been silently milked each morning by its neighbouring litter of piglets.

Games and festivities

Cotswold customs started on 5th January — old Christmas Eve. This was the traditional wassailing night. The wassail bowl was a heady brew of hot ale, spices and roasted apples in a huge bowl made of the maple tree, just as in the old wassailing song. The word itself comes from the Anglo-Saxon toast of 'Be of good Cheer', and it was as wishing health and prosperity to the visited farms and big houses of the neighbourhood that the song developed. Reward for such bucolic blessing came in the shape of mincepies, more warming brew and pennies in the pocket. Wassailing the apple trees to ensure a good crop the next season is still carried out in isolated pockets of the western edge.

Twelfth night

Back to the misty past for celebrations of the end of Christmas festivities. Emma Dent of Sudeley Castle wrote in Victorian times of the fun they had at Twelfth Night when 'characters were drawn' to discover who was to be Queen Pea and King Bean as the master and mistress of ceremonies for the night. She referred to the ladies' characters being drawn out of 'a good old-fashioned reticule' and the mens' from a hat. 'I remember on one occasion when it was my luck to draw the queen, the rapture of having a glittering crown placed on my head, and walking up and down the dancing room with my also glitteringly crowned young king'. Equally by chance and fun was the cutting of the specially baked Twelfth Cake, the finding of the pea and bean inside being the orb and sceptre for the night's reigning monarchs.

The lottery of beans (dried of course) was enjoyed in the Cotswolds during the Roman occupation. The sedate dancing at Sudeley Castle was a timid echo of the no doubt bawdy Saturnalia celebrated in Roman times. Masters and slaves changed roles for the festivities — a custom found dating back to the Middle Ages and revived in the Tudor revelries. The ashen faggot, a bundle of ash logs bound with a withy or hazel bond, was ceremoniously burnt in the large open fireplaces — as each bond popped open another toast was drunk. Some places exercised this ritual on the boundary of farm land to propitiate the fortunes for ensuing crops.

Festive food

Festivals meant food, and each had its own special dish associated with the celebration — such as the harvest loaf shaped like a sheaf of wheat. These out-of-the-ordinary treats leavened the monotonous diet on which the large families existed, and were looked forward to for months. The even leaner period of Lent was relieved by simnel cake and frumenty which Cotswold families enjoyed on Mothering Sunday. An ecclesiastical celebration of centuries, when small communities visited the Mother Church of the diocese, it became the day when servants were allowed time off to participate and the offspring visited their own mothers on that day. Girls who had been in service, to prove their training in the culinary arts, baked a simnel cake, fruit filled and topped and sandwiched with marzipan; this later became adopted as a traditional Easter cake. Mothers, in turn, baked their visiting children frumenty. The recipes vary a little from area to area, but traditionally it was served as a pudding with whey strained off home-made cheese, sweetened with honey and accompanied with whatever fruit was available.

Cotswold frumenty

8 ozs wheat grains
3 pints of milk
2 eggs (beaten)
4 ozs mixed raisins and currants
2 ozs sugar
pinch each of ground nutmeg and salt
3 pints water

'Cree' wheat grains by placing them with salt in a casserole dish and stirring into the water. Cover and leave overnight in a slow oven. The next morning there should be no water left and the grains will be well 'plimmed'. Add rest of ingredients except the eggs and cook gently in oven, or on top of range, for another two hours. Add beaten eggs to enrich the frumenty half an hour before end of cooking time.

Whit ales and white pot

He is very good at white pott. By white pott, wee westerners doe meane a great custard or puddinge baked in a bagg, platter, kettle or pan: notinge heerby, a good trencher man, or great eater.

Smythe's description of white pot in Stuart times probably derived from frumenty. Certainly the 'great custard' evolved from early pottage made in the west Cotswolds since time begat Whitsuntide Revels —derived from the Whitsun Ales, the early fund-raising by churches on Patronal Feasts or Wakes, for alms for the poor, helping to maintain the church and clergy and a means of getting rates out of the parishioners in the guise of feasting and junketing. The eighteenth-century county historian, Samuel Rudder, wrote of the Wake or Wap at Randwick thus:

'The Lord of the Manor gives a certain quantity of malt to brew ale to give away at Whitsuntide and a certain quantity of flour to make cakes; everyone who keeps a cow sends curds, others plums [meaning dried fruit], sugar and flour; and the payers to church and poor contribute 6d each towards furnishing out an entertainment, to which every poor person of the parish who comes, has, with a quart of ale, a cake, a piece of cheese, and a cheesecake.'

White Pott, or Put, or Pout or Whipot, according to the village in which it is made varies in consistency as it does in spelling. From a porridgy type of baked custard, to a baked bread and milk sop to a stick-to-your-ribs bread pudding, the one to survive the vagaries of time and taste is the latter —still made for the Randwick Wap, a country fair at which Mock Mayor making is the highlight. This follows the ancient cheese-rolling on the first Sunday in May, when three Double Gloucester cheeses are rolled round the church three times anti-clockwise and carried on a flower-decked litter to the Wap.

Rolling cheeses at Coopers Hill

Cheese rolling

Rolling cheese at Cooper's Hill, above Gloucester, is thought to have derived from establishing grazing rights on the common; another theory is that it is a pagan rite —trying to catch the sun, represented by the cheese — in an annual saturnalia. Again, it is a Whitsuntide custom and still attracts large crowds to witness the bravery and audacity of the contestants hurtling pell-mell down the grassy one-in-one gradient to catch the seven-pound Double Gloucester cheeses. A handbill sent to the city's Town Crier to advertise the event in 1836 conjures up the rustic fun.

Cooper's Hill Weke
to commence on Wits Monday
persisly at 3 o'clock
2 cheese to be ron for
1 Plain Cake to be green for
1 do.do. to be jumpt in the bag for
Horings to be dipt in the toob for
Set of ribbons to be dansed for
Shimey to be ron for
Belt to be rostled for
A bladder of snuff
to be chatred for by hold wimming

Old women no longer chatter for the snuff, shimmies and ribbons and oranges in tubs of brine and grinning through a horse's collar have been replaced by tug-of-war and scrambling for sweets from the maypole.

High jinks at high summer

The woolsack races at Tetbury are often referred to as 'the agony of Gumstool Hill' from the strenuous uphill run that takes place between the pubs — with heavy sacks on the backs of the competitors. It is said to stem from the days when young drovers competed against each other, carrying sacks of Cotswold wool on their back to impress the local girls. This is another Whitsun custom still very much alive today.

Shakespeare wrote of the sheep-shearing feast and the farming calendar was writ big in the lives of this agricultural area. Seed-sowing and harvest played their part, involving whole families in communal feasts and frolics. Pagan ritual and church customs intermingle: Burford revived its medieval dragon procession on Midsummer's Eve and it still weaves its way through the lovely old town on the hill. The once famous Fairford Carnival, instituted as a cycle cavalcade to raise money for its cottage hospital, became 'the greatest show in the west' in its heyday between the world wars. Keyed into the farming cycle, the noble old wagons, barned between hay and corn harvest, were decorated with crepe paper and ingenuity and then processed through the streets, interspersed by bands from far and near. Traction and steam engines have superseded horses and carts, push-bikes and pedestrians in fancy dress, in an annual rally established now for over a quarter of a century. Carnivals, flower shows, garden fetes and village fairs are still very much part of the way of life throughout summer. Mop Fairs, Witney and Cranham Feasts and Stow Horse Fair still carry vestiges of their origins while numerous ploughing matches and agricultural shows demonstrate the old skills and crafts.

The Clipping Ceremony at Painswick is a colourful affair with ancient roots. Often erroneously linked with the trimming of the legendary ninety-nine yews in the churchyard or the shearing of sheep, this clipping comes from the Saxon *ycleping*, meaning embracing. On a Sunday near 19 September, the parishioners embrace their church by joining hands and surging towards it singing the special Clipping Hymn. Girls wear garlands in their hair, and boys sport floral buttonholes. At the end of the service the children are rewarded with a Painswick Bun — extra large, fruity and spicy, made by the local baker — and the vicar is duly presented with two buns in a basket.

Old farm wagons processed through the streets at carnival time.

*This wagon has been
turned into a wedding
cake, complete with hoops
of bells and flowers and a
baker in attendance.*

*Village and townfolk alike
gathered for the summer
fete wearing their best hats.*

The unique Cotswold Olimpicks

I cannot bring my Muse to dropp Vies
Twixt Cotswold, and the Olimpicke exercise:
But I can tell thee Dover, how they Games
Renew the Glories of our blessed James …

Ben Johnson's Epigram to my Joviall Good Friend, Mr Robert Dover, on his inauguration of hunting and dancing on Cotswold, is one of many poetic praises brought together in *Annalia Dubrensia*, published in 1636, saluting the originator of the Cotswold Olimpicks. Whether he founded the games, which were to bear his name and put the hill on which they were played on the map for all time, or whether he revived a more ancient meeting of sportsmen, is not easily discovered. However they came into being it was Robert Dover, a barrister who settled variously at Saintbury and Chipping Campden in the north Cotswolds, who, with the permission of James I, instituted a custom in the Cotswold calendar which managed to survive the changing fashions of fourteen reigns, despite an inevitable gap during the Civil War when Puritan kill-joys banned all festivities and anything that seemed like a jolly.

The Games — to which Slender refers: 'How does your fallow greyhound, Sir? I heard he was outrun on Cotsall' — were well known to Shakespeare and links between wrestling and coursing in a couple of his plays can be made to the activities on the hill above Chipping Campden, a plateau steeply pitched from the fruit vale of Evesham. The dominant feature is the figure of Dover himself, mounted on a fine horse and arrayed in the king's cast-off clothes — obtained for him by his friend Endymion Porter, Groom of the Royal Bedchamber. Horse racing, cudgel playing, shin-kicking and backswords, sports and feasting and music and dancing were introduced in the programme by the firing of guns from a model castle.

Robert Dover settled in the Cotswolds in 1611 and the games meeting, which today still bears his name, probably began the following year.

Dover's Meeting
1819.

The celebrated Sports of this highly distinguished Festival (which have been the Admiration of all honest, learned, and well-disposed Britons for upwards of two Centuries, and which are now patronised and esteemed by all noble, brave, and liberal minded Men, who have a sincere and true regard for their native Country,) will commence as follows :

On THURSDAY in the WHITSUNTIDE WEEK,
UPON THAT HIGHLY ADMIRED AND MOST DELIGHTFUL SPOT
Called,

DOVER'S HILL,
NEAR CHIPPING CAMPDEN, GLOUCESTERSHIRE,
THERE WILL BE A PURSE OF
TWENTY GUINEAS,
To be played for at Backswords,
By Men, as shall be agreed upon, to begin play at three o'clock in the Afternoon;
TO BE SUCCEEDED BY
Wrestling for a Silver Cup, or three Guineas,
BY NINE MEN ON A SIDE; ALSO, THERE WILL BE SEVERAL
HANDSOME PRIZES TO BE DANCED FOR,
LIKEWISE VERY LIBERAL PRIZES WILL BE GIVEN FOR
JINGLING, BOWLING, LEAPING, and RUNNING in SACKS,
Together with a Multiplicity of the Noted Olympic Games and National Sports, peculiar to this ancient Festival, which cannot be detailed in a Bill.

And on FRIDAY, the Sports will commence with a

Horse   Race,

FOR A SWEEPSTAKES OF FIVE GUINEAS EACH, WITH THIRTY-FIVE GUINEAS ADDED THERETO;

For Horses not thorough bred, which have never started against a thorough bred one, or won a Plate, and which have been Hunted the last season, in either of the Counties of *Gloucester, Warwick, Worcester, Oxford, or Hereford*; to be bona fide the property of the person naming. Four years Old, to carry 10 stone and 5lb. Five years Old, 10 stone and 7lb. Six years Old and Aged, 11 stone and 2lb. the best of Three 2 Mile and a Quarter Heats; the Horses to be named to the Clerk of the Course, at the House of Mr. Andrews, the Old King's Arms Inn, in Chipping Campden aforesaid, on or before Saturday, the 29th day of May preceding the Race, as the Subscription must finally close on that day, for it will be useless to attempt to enter a Horse after the day fixed; (a Certificate of the Age and Qualification must be produced if required; three Subscribers or no Race; all Stakes to be paid to the Clerk of the Course, or to the Steward, by twelve o'clock on the day of running. To be followed by a numberless variety of

The famed Cotswold Sports and Manly Diversions,
NOT EASILY TO BE DESCRIBED.

N. B. The Horses will be started precisely at four o'clock in the Afternoon, and if any dispute arise, the same shall be finally settled by the Steward, (who will be appointed by the Gentlemen of Chipping Campden, at their Meeting, previous to the Race, as usual.) All Dogs seen on the Course will be destroyed. No person will be permitted to erect a Booth, or to sell any kind of Liquor or Beverage without previously paying one Guinea to the Conductor of the Sports. A main of Cocks will be fought each Morning in Campden, as usual. Also, excellent Ordinaries, Balls, Plays, and Concerts each day. Tickets for the Steward's Ball, on Friday evening, at the Noel Arms Inn, Ladies' 5s. Gentlemen's 10s. 6d. to be had at the Bar. On Saturday a Wake will be held in Campden, with a variety of Amusements, as usual.

R. ANDREWS, Clerk.

Chipping Campden, April 14th, 1819.

Stratford, Printed at Barnacle's Letter-press and Copper-plate Office, where Engraving is executed in the best style of Workmanship and Books neatly bound.

Spectacular in its elevated position on the hilltop, the Games attracted nobility and rascality alongside the local folk. Richard Graves, whose home was at nearby Mickleton, depicted the common rustics thus:

'There were a great many swains in their holiday clothes, with their belts and silk handerchiefs; and nymphs in straw hats and tawdry ribbands, flaunting, ogling and coqueting (in their rustic way) with as much alacrity as any of the gay flutterers in the mall'.

His literary preacher, Geoffrey Wildgoose, watching where 'a Holland shift' was to be run for by six young ladies lined up 'before the whole assembly in a dress hardly reconcileable to the rules of decency', leapt on to his hamper and exhorted the crowd to shun 'these anti-Christian recreations'. Unfortunately for the mild Methodist Wildgoose, he was assumed to be a mountbank plying his quack cures and was pelted by orange peel, clods of earth and horse-dung and driven from the hill — 'Thus unsuccessfully ended Wildgoose's first effort towards reforming the world'.

And the Games live on to this day. Under the Robert Dover's Games Society, the Cotswold Olimpicks marry the past with the present: tableaux and demonstrations, displays and games conclude with a grand finale at which the Scuttlebrook Wake Queen lights the bonfire, signalling a fireworks display, and ends with a torchlight procession down to the old market town for dancing in the square.

Christmas Mummers

In comes I, old Father Christmas, Christmas or not,
I hope old Father Christmas will never be forgot:
Roast beef, plum pudding and mince pies,
Never did old Father Christmas like these better than I.
A room, a room, a gallant room and give us room to rhyme,
For we to show our bold activities this merry Christmas time

So begins the Snowshill version of many Cotswold Mummers plays which once threaded their weird and magical thread into Christmastide. The play itself originated at Blockley and was taught to the young men of Snowshill around the turn of the century. In true oral tradition, the plays were not written down but learnt from generation to generation. The parts vary from village to village in the character of the representation of evil, and tended to portray the contemporary bad man of the day — so Turkish Knight and Napoleon crept into some versions, to be fought by compatible combatants, who always won the day as good triumping over evil. The spirit of Father Christmas sets the seasonal tone and is the introduction to the folk play.

Never designed as a stage set, Mummers plays appear unintelligible and nonsensical in dialogue. The essential character is the doctor 'who kills more than he cures, but can deal with the itch, the impsy, pimpsy, palsy and gout, pains within and pains without'. His main function is to bring to life the slain evil character, representing the revival of the dying year and so linking its origins to pagan fertility rites. Belzebub, the name for the devil, appears in many versions and is the one to have survived in the few still to be found in the Cotswolds. Some ten versions were in existence fifty years ago — today only the Gloucester City, Waterley Bottom and Marshfield — distinctive in their all paper costumes — perform regularly, with a handful of revivals intermittently.

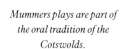

Mummers plays are part of the oral tradition of the Cotswolds.

Painswick Bow Wows

Puppy Dog Pie became a traditional dish served at Painswick Feast — the Sunday of the Clipping Ceremony. The pies were of apple, with the pie funnel shaped like a small dog, according to Mrs Peggy Perrin whose family shop sold the china pie funnels. The tale of the Painswick Bow Wows, which is still the local name given to native Painswickians, was told me by Mrs Perrin 'who had it from her father, who had it from his grandfather' — in the manner in which Beatrix Potter first heard the tale of the Tailor of Gloucester on her visit to Harescombe.

As was the way with neighbouring villages, the Painswick boys had a long-standing feud with the youths of Whitehill. Superiority was fought for every Saturday night on the hill — until one night the Painswick fellows called a truce and, as a token towards their intent to keep peace with their adversaries, invited them to a feast the following week. After enjoying the spread of meat pies made specially for them, the Whitehill boys were told they had eaten the dogs of Painswick — untrue, but an insult strong enough to renew the weekly scraps. The tale has been nurtured through the years and has outlived the tradition of the pie.

Michaelmas Goose

> *Whoever eats goose on Michaelmas Day*
> *Shall never lack money for his debts to pay*

The old song dates back to the time when tenants paid their Michaelmas rents, marking the third quarter of the year, and the rights of common land leazing for the cottager's geese. A goose at Michaelmas is less fatty than at Christmas and was stuffed with forcemeat and prunes as in medieval times.

Jubilee ox roast at Bisley.

May Queen and her attendants enthroned on a wagon for May Day celebrations at Bledington in 1939.

Floral Festival at Chipping Campden, with the town's Morris Men, in 1896.

Harvest fields were busy in pre-machinery days. Whole families went harvesting in some form or other, mothers helped fathers with the actual work of stooking the sheaves — and children played in and around the golden strawed wigwams.

Harvesting by Custom

When ye reap the harvest of your land, thou shalt not wholly reap the corners of thy field, neither shalt thou gather the gleanings of thy harvest.

The law of Moses was carried out in the Cotswolds into the post-war era until giant combine harvesters reaped the corners and destroyed this ancient charity. From the gleanings — or leazings as they are called locally — a couple of bags of flour would be milled at the local mill and stored in the cottage 'back place', an insurance in kind against empty tables in the winter. School Log Books give references to 'large numbers of children away leazing after harvest'; monitors also escaped their duties to gather in this scriptural harvest home. The townsfolk obviously did not cling to the rural rights as long as their country cousins as an entry in Powells School at Cirencester for 1891 states 'there is now a contempt for gleaning'. Barley, once commonly grown on the Cotswolds, was gleaned as much as wheat and made barley 'skorkers' in the lean years of the Agricultural Depression — a kind of scone, it replaced bread in the humblest homes.

The harvest stook was a good place to hide behind for a quick cuddle, giggle or swig out of the stone cider jar. Young boys thrashed around with long sticks beating the rabbits before the binder, quick-witted and accurate-eyed youngsters bagged a couple for the family cooking and school holidays were timed to the harvest. Baskets or frails — rush-woven flat bags — carried dinner: a 'snowl' of bread and cheese, perhaps a hefty lump of fruit cake, mutton dormers, (a kind of meat patty), bottles of cold tea or home-brewed cordials. My great grand-mother was ingenious at devising non-alcoholic harvest drinks, an enthusiasm not shared by my grandfather who added a note to the receipts that Cotswold barley could be brewed into 'proper' harvest ale for '£1 per hundred gallons'!

Granny Lewis's harvest drinks

Stokos: Mix 6 ozs freshly ground oatmeal, fine as flour, with enough cold water straight from the pump, to make a thin cream. Stir in 6 ozs fine white sugar, one thinly sliced lemon and add 1 gallon freshly boiled water.
(Cost: one shilling per 5 gallons).

Cokos: Mix 4 ozs freshly ground oatmeal, 4 ozs cocoa powder and 6 ozs fine white sugar with a little cold water. Pour on a gallon of fresh boiled water, stirring all the time. Take to the fields in a stone jar. (Cost: 4d per gallon).

Hopkos: Boil ½ oz of hops and ½ oz bruised ginger in 1½ gallons of water over a brisk fire for 25 minutes. Add 1 lb best brown sugar and boil for a further 10 minutes. Strain through scalded muslin into a cask while hot. Store in a cold cellar and take to the fields in a stone jar. Dried horehound may be used instead of hops.
(Cost: 3d per gallon).

Nutting

A good nut year, a good baby year

Holy Rood Day, 14 September, signalled the start of Nutting Week, when villages around Cirencester Park were invited by Lord Bathurst to nut freely from his woods. School Log Books again record the custom with Daglingworth, Sapperton, Cirencester and Coates gathering in the autumn harvest until quite recent years. Avening celebrated its feast on the first Sunday after the 14th, its church being dedicated to the Holy Rood (or Cross).

Before the days of giant combine harvesters gleanings (or leazings) were left in the corners and edges of the fields for local folk to gather.

The last working team of oxen in England drawing hay at Cirencester Park. The boy was Ted Smith who, at the age of twelve, left school to work for forty-eight years on the Bathurst Estate with the animals he so loved. Jimmy and Joey, the last pair of oxen to be used on the farm when working oxen had become a rarity, appeared on television, films and shows — along with Ted, their trainer and handler.

The noble game of cricket

... which is not only our national game, but is the king of games, is a pastime for the working classes. A sport that is not confined to the rich or poor, but is joined in by all classes, who on the cricket field are on the same level

So spake the colossus of cricket himself — the legendary W G Grace, who bestrode the playing fields of England taking the name of Gloucestershire into the history of the game itself by starting the County matches in 1871.

Of all the pastimes indulged in by Cotsallers throughout the ages, it is cricket which has endured the vagaries of fashion to become the cornerstone of our culture. 'What is human life, but a game of cricket?' asked the third Duke of Dorset in an essay of 1797, and literature has been punctuated with references to the game, with memorable matches created by the pen of Dickens and J Arthur Gibbs — the latter's description of village cricket would have been as a participant as well as writer. Gibbs was an enthusiastic cricketer both for the Cotswold village team in his home patch at Ablington in the Coln Valley and for the MCC. His notebooks are filled with jottings on how to improve cricket fields and a slim volume on their creation and maintenance was his first publication at a time when a hardbound book could safely be embossed with its price of one shilling and sixpence in gold on the cover.

The Cotswolds can lay claim, albeit somewhat tenuously, to the origination of this noble game. Folklore fancies it having started from shepherds swiping at stray stones with their crooks upturned 'in an idle hour' — but then the self-swain of the sheepwalks is credited with having chiselled out the escarpment face to create the wondrous stone curiosity of the Devil's Chimney overlooking Cheltenham — in yet another indolent period. Certainly pictorial evidence points to

early forms of bat and ball games being played with a curved stave rather like a modern hockey stick. The earliest illustration of anything resembling a cricketing batsman is the stained glass rondel in Gloucester Cathedral circa 1350.

John Smyth, steward of the Hundred of Berkeley, and brought up in the Berkeley family, was a contemporary of Shakespeare and lived at North Nibley. He was an avid chronicler of his time and so it is with some confidence that we can turn to his manuscript of 1639 in which he describes the pastimes of the day.

'...in the hilly or Cotteswold part, doe witness the inbred delight that both gentry, yeomanry, rascallity, boyes and children doe take in a game called Stoball,
the play whereat each child of 12 years old, can
I suppose as well describe as my selfe. And not
a sonne of mine but at 7 was furnished with his
double stoball staves, and a gamster thereafter.'
Two references point to this Stoball being an early form of cricket: firstly, in the Tate Gallery, London paintings of Georgian cricket show distinctly a two-stump wicket; secondly, betting was included in the 'Laws of the Noble Game of Cricket' and the players were known as gamesters. So the 'double staves' and 'gamster' of John Smyth's record are borne out. A later topographical writer, John Aubrey, elucidates on the game of Stoball:

'Stoball-play is peculiar to north Wilts, south
Gloucestershire and a little part of Somerset near
Bath. They smite the ball, stuffed very hard with
quills and covered with soale leather, with a
staffe, commonly made of withy, about 3 feet and
a halfe long ... A Stobball ball is of about four
inches diameter, and as hard as stone.'
The leather-covered hard ball and bat of willow could not be anything else but the tools of cricket, and the fortunes of the local team are a matter of great parochial pride — nothing epitomizes England at her rural best than a cricket match in timeless progress.

The official records verify that the game was introduced in the county 'for a purse'.

Gloucester 1729
The Weekly Journal or British Gazetteer announced in September — the 22nd instant will be played in the Town-ham of this city, by eleven men of a side a game of cricket, for upwards of 20 guineas.

Cirencester 1769
The young gentlemen of that place are introducing the manly game of cricket into this county, where it has been hitherto unknown. Some excellent matches have been lately played there for considerable sums.

Cheltenham 1805
Venue of Brig. Gen. Clavering and ten others v Rev Pulter and ten others. (A cricket club was formed in 1833.)

Clifton Club v Bath Club 1819
...many distinguished themselves, and while the spectators were gratified at the skill and science evinced in the course of the game, they were no less struck by the harmony and decorum that prevailed. As we have seldom had an opportunity of witnessing this game played in strict conformity with the established rules, it may easily be believed much curiosity was aroused ... this manly game will meet with every encouragement from the numerous gentlemen residing in or near this city.

*Abbey's Artists
Club XI
in 1903*

*The colours of the Club
were red, black and white,
on Abbey's suggestion. Red
represented colour in art,
and black and white the
other branches.*

*Left to right (back row, standing)
Arnesby Brown, Henry Ford, Gerald F Chowne, L D Luard, Arthur Studd,
Sir Reginald Blomfield (well known architect of the Menin Gate Memorial in Ypres), G Hillyard Swinstead
Front row (seated)
G Gascoigne, Edwin A Abbey, Walter John James (later Lord Northbourne), Mrs Abbey, L C Nightingale*

The picturesque thatched cricket pavilion, set on Cotswold stone staddles - to keep it raised above the low-lying riverian field - was given to the village of Stanway by J M Barrie.

The turn of the century saw the formation of other professional group clubs, including the famous Authors' XI, for which J M Barrie was chiefly responsible.

Playing out time in an awkward light: by Frank Batson. Like most of the team he was a Royal Academician — this painting, an oil on canvas, is unusual in cricket pictures as it depicts the bowler seen through the eyes of the batsman, on the cricket field at Morgan Hall.

It hangs in the Long Room at the famous Trent Bridge Pavilion of Nottinghamshire County Cricket Club.

Artists of cricket

There could hardly have been a more distinguished cricket XI than the Artists Cricket Club, instituted in 1898 by the famous American artist Edwin A Abbey. Membership was restricted to painters, sculptors and architects at an annual subscription of five shillings. Abbey visited the Cotswolds several times in the previous decade and used features in the Tudor Swan Inn at Lechlade and Buscot Rectory as background in his paintings. It was while he was in the north Cotswolds at Broadway with Frank Millet that he 'first seriously attacked the problem of oil painting' and met his future wife.

The Abbeys moved to Morgan Hall, an Elizabethan dower house in Fairford, in 1891 and built what was described as the largest studio in England for a painter. A frequent visitor was fellow American and famed novelist, Henry James, who, in one of his letters wrote of Mrs Abbey's fresh laid eggs 'better the British hen than the American eagle'.

In 1898 Abbey laid out a cricket ground 'with the advice from a neighbouring cricketer and friend, author of that admirable book, *A Cotswold Village*'. The friend was J Arthur Gibbs. Sadly, he died before he could have enjoyed the fun and games held annually at Morgan Hall. Abbey wrote of the trouble in maintaining the pitch for the 'week'.

'...the weight of the roller slid back this morning and nearly hung the horse. He broke one of the iron shafts. The lawn mower he was to have towed hadn't arrived. He was a hired steed and if he had died no doubt he would have turned out very valuable. The boy who lies on the ground is of no value.'

G Hillyard Swinstead spoke of the Artists' Week with equal humour.

'The Club was founded just before midnight in a cloud of tobacco smoke on 20th July 1898. Our ages ranged between 30 and 50 and we played a solid week's cricket, putting up a good fight every time.

Luncheon was held in the great 70 feet studio, where the teams, together with Mrs Abbey (who was the only lady allowed in the sacred sect, with the odd exception of Lord St Aldwyn's daughters, the Ladies Hicks-Beach) the umpires, scorers and two or three stray guests. We sat down at one long table on all sorts of seats and benches ranging in period from Henry IV to Victoria. A more unusual and picturesque cricket luncheon never was and very little art talk was indulged in, although five or six huge paintings of "The Quest for the Holy Grail" stood silently around. The only brush that he (Abbey) touched during the

---

The following season reaped the following results:

1899

April 25
Varnishing Day Match v Chelsea Arts Club.— Won.

April 26
E A Abbey's Fairford XI v Chelsea Arts Club.— Lost

May 10
E A Abbey's Fairford XI v Savile Club.— Won

May 19
E A Abbey's Fairford XI v J M Barrie's XI.— Won

June 1
E A Abbey's Fairford XI v Authors,
A Conan Doyle's XI.— Lost

June 15
E A Abbey's Fairford XI v Musicians
(R Kennerley Rumford's XI).— Lost.

---

week was the one belonging to the white wash and pail, when he would mark out the crease.'

Music and charades, eating and talking and smoking filled the evenings. It was said that Abbey (unlike Swinstead) 'was not a great batsman and was exceedingly modest, like all great men. He always insisted on going in last, so was often "not out", but his fielding was excellent'.

The Cotswolds, by dint of being largely in Gloucestershire, tenaciously hold on to the paternity of the great Graces — for all the family were famous cricketers, thanks mainly to the enthusiasm and erudition in the game of their mother, but before that momentous period the little village of Kingscote, near Uley, gave birth to another great cricketing son.

Mr Kingscote comes next, as fine a young man
As ever was built upon nature's best plan;
He stands six feet four - and, what don't often follow,
His leg is a model to form an Apollo.
A fine slashing hitter as ever was found
He sometimes has knocked the ball out of the ground;
An excellent thrower, a hundred yards clear,
And ladies protest that he runs like a deer.

This was how *Scores and Biographies* described Henry Kingscote who, aged twenty-five, was president of the Marylebone Cricket Club in 1827. The Kingscote Club boasted a 250-run victory over the MCC in 1871.

Other great names have made their mark in the annals of 'Cricket's manly toil', as Byron described the game. When Charlie Barnett put down his bat to take up arms for his country in the Second World War, the local paper (which in line with other newspapers and magazines had been warned not to give names or movements of anyone in the services as potential 'useful information to the enemy') gave its message loud and clear: If our great cricketer is as handy with a gun as he is with a bat — Hitler had better look out!

AT WORK

Oldborough Farm, prior to 1915 when Mr Hodgkins [centre of haystack] died. Mrs Hodgkins, [extreme right] with the help of her two sons,
Jack [extreme left] and Bert [with the horse], went on after her husband's death to run the farm until she died at the age of eighty.

Places of work

Quenington paper mill

Mills for many uses: paper making

Mills on the Cotswolds at Domesday were cornmills serving the immediate community for grinding the harvest into flour for the daily bread. The medieval wool trade made use of the water-driven millworks to power the ancillary industries of fulling and dyeing. As the decline in the cloth-making slowed the old mill wheels into depression, the expansion of trade in other light industries turned them again for new purpose. As yet unpolluted by heavy industry, the Cotswold rivers and streams with clean pure water from the springs that fed them, adapted readily to the new manufactory of paper making. From the 1750s some estimated three dozen paper mills came into being. For some, as at Postlip,

paper making was initially a winter-time industry, the mill reverting to grinding corn in the summer time. Postlip therefore kept one of its three paper mills as a dual-purpose mill busy for a hundred years until it went over to paper making full-time in 1850.

> Rags make Paper,
> Paper makes Money,
> Money makes Banks,
> Banks make Loans,
> Loans make Beggars,
> Beggars make Rags.

Salutory philosophy indeed by that ubiquitous author Anon, whose pen has been responsible for so many of our best and tersest verse.

Rags were the principal raw material for paper making until 1950 and among the journal entries of 1878 are prices for bags of rags of, print, blues, blacks, whites, thirds and seconds, and twenty-two bags of 'old Pickens' were bought for twenty-seven shillings. The roads and paths and field trackways from Winchcombe some mile and a bit away following the little river, and those running over Cleeve Hill to Cheltenham, have been trodden, traversed and crisscrossed for centuries as cartloads of bulging bales of rags bumped their way to the mill; millworkers trudged back and fro through the seasons and wagonloads packed with paper left the picturesque valley of the wolds.

It would seem that paper making at Quenington was also a seasonal industry as, according to a charge sheet of 1830, a James Silk was transported for seven years for wilfully and maliciously destroying a threshing machine, the property of Joshua Corby Radway, paper maker. The winding hill leading down to the Coln waters which powered the paper mill perpetuates that period in its name of Rag Hill.

Only the name remains of former paper-making enterprises in farms and cottages at Stanway and Barrington. Guns Mill, near Gloucester, was a former forge and turned to paper making by Joseph Lloyd about 1743. A bill for paper made at the mill in 1827 gives the prices of:

2 reams fine copy at 30 shillings
1 ream briefs at 33 shillings
1 ream thick wove letter at £1

Of the paper-making industries, only Postlip remains. Idyllically sited, with a millpond which can provide 80,000 gallons an hour and on foundations of a mill dating back to Saxon times, the purity of the water gains mystical properties by 'running against the sun' of the little Isbourne, one of the two streams on the confluence of which the mill stands — it is a magical place. William Gates Adlard kept a silver cup at the well for passers-by to quench their thirst and have a wish. If travellers passed by at midnight they might be joined by the little stone figure of Sir William de Postlip who descends from his perch on the gable of the old tithe barn to drink at Queen Bess's Well.

'At Postlip is one of the most considerable Paper Manufacturers in the Kingdom,' wrote Simon Moreau in 1789. Scale board, made from beechwood, used for band boxes, bookbinding and wig boxes in the reign of George II was taxed at 4s 6d. Coarse linen rags made paste board and 'cordage, tarr ropes and coarse raggs' made white millboard.

A second paper-making enterprise was situated at the east end of the town, called Sudeley Paper Mills —

after the castle neighbour. It was owned by Nathaniel Lloyd, High Bailiff of Winchcombe, who endeavoured to clean up the town by prohibiting the emptying of slops in outside gutters 'a custom they had hitherto enjoyed with impunity'. Obviously the slops were never used in paper dyes as in the older methods of wool dyeing or tanneries; recipes for coloured papers do not include such a lowly ingredient. The 'receipts' are fascinating:

Orange
Mix 6 lb Sugar of Lead in half a bucket of hot water, also 3 lb of Bichrome in another half bucket. Mix the two together and when thoroughly mixed and dissolved in Sugar of Lead buckets, put in engine and in half an hour add 1 ½ lb of Birds Albert Lake. July 18th 1864

Caustic Ash
Take 112 lb Soda Ash and 64 lb clear Lime. Slake the lime in the ash kettle and when fallen let in your water to the soda ash and apply steam. When all boiled into milk of lime put in the ash, keeping it well stirred, until all dissolved. Should it not be caustic enough add lime, the liquer will then be fit for use. By making your ash caustic it will answer your purpose much better.
This receipt refers only to very dirty rags, not to Esparto. 1864

Esparto is a grass which superseded rags as the main raw material. Coloured blotting paper was a well established line at that time, including a black blotting paper which was used by banks in an attempt to foil any would-be law-breakers. Journal entries for 1878 include '£62 paid for a brown horse, six years sound, called Jolly; and 'an old horse' sold for £7. An elm tree, from G Lane, measuring 94 ft 6 ins cost 6 guineas and forty-five yards of wagon rope 7s 11d'. A new

brass dandy roll appears among the costs of lime and stone, alum and tallow, potash and nut oil.

Eleanor Adlard, in her little history of Postlip Mill, gives a charming word portrait of a Dandy Roll maker:

... wearing a tall silk hat, having fortified himself for the walk up, [George Tovey] would steer a somewhat uncertain course carrying his precious rolls through Winchombe up to the Mills.

She also describes the travelling basket-makers, 'who arrived to cut, soak, and strip the withies grown by the ponds and weave them into the great two-handled baskets to carry pulp, paper, or rags.' Dandy rolls are wire rollers which imprint designs or watermarks on the paper while it is still wet. Water-marks are moulds stitched to the outside of the dandies.

Like other locally-owned industries in small communities, Postlip Mill owners ploughed part of the profits into philanthropic causes; the Adlards who bought the estate in 1849 founded charities, built almshouses and cottages for the workers and gave the church financial support. A Sick Society was founded in 1868; members subscribed sixpence fortnightly on receipt of wages. The rules excluded payment to those 'whose illness is produced through drunkenness, own misconduct, or found to be in a public house gambling or drinking to excess'. A job at the mill was a job for life, a son-following-father, *and* daughter-following-mother tradition; half the workforce of some ninety people at the turn of the century were women.

No longer do the paper makers weave their distinguishing paper hat folded from blue samples; machines have taken over from hand processes and old steam engines; specialist filter papers have replaced the tons of blotting paper once produced but the firm is still owned by the same company and under the watershed of the north Cotswold Hills all is still as rural a scene as ever.

Cottage shops

Setting up cottage shops required a licence as this little document states:

'I, Anthony Weatherstone of Windrush in the county of Glocester do hereby make entry of two rooms in my dwelling house situate at Windrush aforesaid for the purpose of selling and storing of coffee, teas, tobacco and snuff for sale.
Witness my hand this 3rd day of August 1816'

Windrush village shop accounts for 1853 give the prices of the only basic foods supplied to a Frederick Durham in 1853:

April 26

3 loaves 1s 7½d
2 lb cheese 1s 4d
2 lb bacon 1s 4d
½ lb butter 5½d
½ qr flour 3¼d
2 lb lard 1s 6d

In the three months recorded for that customer there was no variation in the foodstuffs bought, only the quantity. The half pound of butter was obviously a luxury as it appears only the once in that period.

The village shop at Coln St Aldwyns belonged to the Independent Co-operative Society and the minutes of a meeting held at the end of January 1876 indicate that it was a matter for the committee to decide the 'stores to be ordered'. It was also muted, on the proposal of Mr Bazley, that Mrs Clarke 'should be asked to furnish the names of tradesmen with whom she is accustomed to deal and who would, in her opinion, be likely to deal liberally with the Society in view of the many stores from the Co-op Wholesale Society arriving in a damaged condition and long delay on the road'.

Elsie Monk, a shop assistant: in Edwardian times young girls were generally expected to go into domestic service and, unless the shop was a family-owned concern, to procure a job there was quite unusual.

FEEDING STUFFS
(RATIONING) ORDER,
1949

Ministry of Agriculture
and Fisheries
Department of
Agriculture for Scotland
Ministry of Food

**PIG OR POULTRY
FOOD COUPON**

THIS COUPON MUST BE
DEPOSITED WITH A
SUPPLIER WITHIN 15
DAYS OF DATE OF ISSUE.
A receipt should be obtained

Date of Issue

If this space is blank the date
of issue is 1st January

MP 460766

⅝ UNIT
PIG OR POULTRY
FOOD

**VALID ONLY FOR
JANUARY**
and next succeeding month

NOT TRANSFERABLE

Available for:

(a) National Pig Food
(see over)

OR

(b) National Poultry Food
(see over)

OR

(c) Cereal Feeding Stuffs
(see over)

This coupon entitles the holder to buy or obtain during the period
named above FIVE EIGHTHS UNIT (the unit being 112 lb., or such
other quantity as may be directed by the Minister of Food) of any
of the feeding stuffs listed on this coupon that may be available.

JANUARY   Form No. P.P.255

*Rationing coupon for pork
and poultry issued in 1949.*

*General grocer's shop
where the display of goods
on the counter almost hides
the shop assistant.*

*A family butcher's with the
Christmas meat hung
outside. A man employed to
ward off dogs with strips of
leather stands in the alley.
He was similarly employed
in summertime to keep flies
at bay with a leather swot.*

Cigarettes and chocolate advertisements dominate the window display in this old shop in Cricklade Street, Cirencester.

Corn mills

Baking the bread from the corn ground at the mill epitomizes the image of country contentment. For years the tall brick chimney and rhythmic clack-clack of the wooden waterwheel at Lower Slaughter symbolized fresh-baked home-milled bread by the Collett family. The unique, warm yeasty aroma was the only direction one needed to seek out the little shop on the corner of this picturesque village.

Water is the picture-postcard feature of nearby Bourton and powered its various mills as part of its working life. The old family firm of Thomas and Henry Wilkins was established in the 1840s. According to the 1851 census, Thomas Wilkins was aged forty-seven, a miller and farmer of a hundred and ten acres employing four labourers. Henry, one of the eight children recorded for that date, was then aged eleven, and was obviously taken into the business on coming of age as Wilkins and Son appear as millers, bakers, corn dealers, grocers, cheese factors and makers, as well as agents for wine and spirits in 1868.

Their ledger commences:

'Uncle William Accounts for Grandfather began on agreement from Stow May Fair 1863 at £3 5s per annum.'

Among the prices given are:

1859 Carter at Brandman 1 sack flour £1 16s
1860 Brindle: 2 bags barley ground 6d
Mrs Bricknell: 5 white Quarterns (loaves) 3s 6d.

A stock list of grocery, including elm boards, two horses, cart, harness, a cow and manure was valued at £558 3s 6d in 1824 which would suggest the valuation of stock in hand was at a change of ownership. Among the stock so meticulously listed were:

Raw sugars, Turkey raisins, Congo tea, currants, green tea, coffee, sealing wax, raisin wine, 'Bast', shag tobacco, treacle, blacking, pepper, Malagas, commercial vinegar, fresh liquer, fifty-one dozen Country candles and seventy dozen London candles, paper, emery sandpaper, Logwood, alum and Fullers earth (obviously for dyeing purposes); sulphur and ochre would have been for shepherd's use; salt petre for home curing of hams. Ten bushels of hemp seed were worth £3 7s. Three hundredweight of cheese were valued at £10 7s, considerably cheaper weight for weight than the equivalent stock of starch.

Miller's wagon at Bourton on the Water.

Mr Raven delivers bread by pony and trap. Today his grandson continues the family tradition, baking bread in Victorian ovens.

Ale and breweries

'Item that alle maner of brewers that brueth ale to sale that they brew good ale and holsom for mannys body not rede nor ropyng, and that they sel under the heresyff a galon of the best ale for a peny, xiii for xii, and of the second ale iii galon for a peny well sodde and skommed.'
Byelaw of 1500: Gloucester Corporation Records

Brewing of both ale and cider has had a long tradition in the Cotswolds. Monasteries, farms and inns and houses, large and small had their own brewhouses for home consumption and all that was needed to sell it was a bunch of greenery displayed outside — this would call the attention of the local ale-taster to the premises to check on quality.

Millers often took up brewing as a sideline, and when this became profitable they turned their corn mills into breweries. Godsell's at Stroud is first mentioned as a cloth mill in 1496. There was a malt house in 1827 and Godsells was a household name for brewing from the mid 1850s. Taken over by the Stroud Brewery, it closed down its vats in 1967.

The only brewery to remain in production on the hills is Donnington, near Stow-on-the-Wold. In the most picturesque pocket of the wooded wolds, the stone-built mill, which dates back to 1291 and has served both the woollen and corn milling industries, relied entirely on the waterwheel power until about thirty years ago. The wheels still turn the silvery waters where waterfowl dip and dive between the flower-fringed banks of the pond, but they are supplemented now by engine power.

Mr Claude Arkell maintains the tradition of brewing real ale in the beautiful brewery which his grandfather started in 1865 and the family supplies its own seventeen pubs in the area. 'Originally, they were all within fifteen miles of the brewery, which is about the distance a horse-drawn dray could travel there and back in a day. Some of the workers spend their lifetime here and all are fully conversant with the processes,' he says. The water is drawn from the crystal springs which feed the pretty river Dikler and only natural ingredients are used.

It seems extraordinary that a campaign for real ale had to re-educate the ale-drinking populace to the stuff our forefathers enjoyed; but, as with all small-in-comparison enterprises, the scale imposes its own exclusiveness — and in this case it is the Cotswolds who hold the privilege.

Donnington brewery.

Traditional horse brewer's dray.

Advertising locally brewed beer to help the war effort.

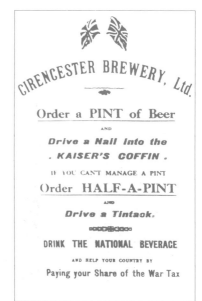

CIRENCESTER BREWERY, Ltd.

Order a PINT of Beer
AND
Drive a Nail into the
. KAISER'S COFFIN .
IF YOU CAN'T MANAGE A PINT
Order HALF-A-PINT
AND
Drive a Tintack.
DRINK THE NATIONAL BEVERAGE
AND HELP YOUR COUNTRY BY
Paying your Share of the War Tax

Farming and crops

The diary of J S Calvertt of Leafield Farm in Oxfordshire gives an interesting glimpse at farming in the south-eastern corner of the Cotswolds and the social life of the gentlemen farmers of the day. Calvertt moved to Leafield in 1876.

Bedecked and beribboned with traditional brasses, the noble heavy horses stir memories of life behind the plough.

1876

February 9
Snowy morning, counted 37 pigeons in the dovecot.

April 12
10 women picking stones off the grass lands and clovers. 1s a day.

April 16
Attended Leafield Church for the first time. The Revd Lee is Vicar. John and Robert walked round by High Lodge and the rough Old Forest in the afternoon.

April 18
Ploughed road sides and trimmed brambles off the walls from entrance gates to Ascott parish. Cutting up the ant hills on the Langley grass and Home Close as well as picking off the stones.

April 21
Mr and Mrs Savidge and Mrs Abraham tea'd and spent the evening, Mrs A is an acquaintance of the famous preacher, Spurgeon. Three horsemen left because I would not give 15s instead of 14s per week.

April 22
Re-breasting, the 14 ploughs with short breasts.

June 4
Drove Alice and Elizabeth to Shipton-under-Wychwood in the evening and heard Revd Barter: service performed as stylish as at St Paul's.

June 9
Leafield Holiday today and tomorrow, scarcely any work done till next day, as is quite the custom.

July 7
Carrying manure out on clover land, for wheat, instead of carrying clovers.

July 11
Shot a magpie and 3 rabbits in Priest Grove at 5½am. Finished clover carrying and very relieved and pleased, I feel, having secured about 180 acres of clovers, sainfoin and meadow, in good condition, and probably less expense, than ever I may expect again for years.
Mr Shillingford, Witney, bought wool yesterday, 33s per tod.

July 12
Commenced skerrying turnips on Shipton field and Boynel Gardens !!! with Mr Heanley's old skerries !!!!

September 25
To Burford Hiring Fair — hired John Carter for shepherd and two married and one single carter.

October 9
Sold an old horse £6 15s 6d and a giddy lamb 27s 6d at Shipton auction. Dores plashing hedge by Shipton Road and leaving a few hawthorn bushes for ornament — 19 chains completed for £2 — which is cheap!

November 1
Commenced threshing wheats and barley for a fortnight two days ago. Attended Mr Iorns, furniture sale at South Lawn, and sent some of Mr Heanley's furniture. Brought away a cart, wheelbarrow and ladder £7 19s 3d. First black ice over the Langley Ponds.

Steam threshing at Beacon Farm in about 1906.

An old newspaper cutting shows a Victorian design steam plough with a cable drum girdling the boiler.

Butcher Arthur Woodward took pride in selecting his beef 'on the hoof' and always boasted the Fatstock Show prizewinner for display in his shop window. He is seen here with stockman Mr Boddington and a prize bull.

November 4

Attended Leafield School meeting (yesterday) —agreed to pay 3d rate. By rail to Oxford Market. Sold to Mr Gourn, Birmingham, 90 qrs barley at 36s. Dined at the Roebuck Hotel. Mr Castle in the chair. Also Mr Butt and Skerry 23 qrs at 30s; 55½ qrs wheat to Mr Gourn at 48s. Alice, Elizabeth and John were driven to meet the hounds at Blenheim and were very pleased with all they witnessed — one of the most stylish Meets in England! Drag-harrowed twice, 95 acres —fallows for turnips ploughed early.

1877

February 27

Rode to Taynton and called on Mr Matthews who showed me the road to Coln St Aldwyns near Hatherop Castle, where we met the Prince of Wales, Earl Shannon and the Vale of White Horse Hounds —trotted off to Bibury Race course Gorse and ran across the country nearly to Jolly's Gorse, found and ran into the Bradwell Covers, where I left them and reached home at 2 pm. Changed horses and rode to Heythrop and joined Mr Brassey and party coursing at 3½ pm. Dined at Mr Blake's and home again at 1.30 am. Bought 20 qrs sainfoin seed of Mr Bulford who was coursing judge, 19 of us dined. The Prince of Wales looked jolly and well, and appeared in sound, robust health.

March 17

Charlbury is a very old, badly built stone village, and Quakers are said to abound.

Pitch and toss: haymaking at Coneygre Farm, Quenington.

—they really seem more dissatisfied now with 10 shillings than last year with 7. Two of the principal farmers very indiscreetly reduced their labourers a few weeks ago to 9 shillings, on which they struck and came to the house. My mother spoke to two of them and they all behaved very quietly. When my brother came he settled that while the neighbouring villages paid 10 shillings, this should also, but we expect more discontent as at harvest time the men want 15 shillings, which the farmers will not give. The public houses here do a vast deal of mischief — some of the most troublesome people in the parish are however disposed of for the present — either transported, in prison or run away.

(Signed) I M Hicks Beach'

Two years later, John Keble wrote to his brother Thomas, Vicar of Bisley:

'... We are going to get rid of all our Coln beer-houses in regard to which Squire Beach uttered a sentiment today which struck me as genuine True Blue. I said, "We must make up our mind to lose a vote or two," and he said, "O, never mind the votes as long as we are doing right." '

J Arthur Gibbs voiced his fears for the drift from the land as the Victorian era drew to a close and the depression bit deeper into the countryside. In his *Cotswold Village* he pleaded, 'Let the Cotswold labourer realise that to work on the land, ploughing and reaping, summer and winter, seedtime and harvest, come weal, come woe, is no mean destiny for an honest man...'

While, in his small pocket notebook J Arthur Gibbs pencilled his aide memoir:

'John Brown lives on £10 a year; Trinder and his 21 children must not be left out of C. Village — our carter, Trinder, is a cheery fellow — think of all the offspring there will be. He says he has always got by somehow. The man is a hero, as are these honest labourers hereabouts.'

Agricultural riots

A half century before, when the Cotswolds witnessed its share of the agricultural riots, John Keble the gentle poet divine came face to face with an angry mob of farm workers marching, destruction bent, towards Fairford where agricultural machinery was being made — and exhibited for sale on the Green.

The mainly local men from his parish at Southrop and Eastleach advanced as he held up his hand to halt them. Equally determined, the quiet curate did not falter in his step and addressed the leader of the mob — and told him his shoes were unfastened, and so might cause him to trip. Completely nonplussed by this consideration rather than the condemnation they expected, the assembly rather sheepishly broke up and returned home.

For all his spiritual commitment, Keble was a deeply political parson. By temperament and up-bringing he was a Tory and in a doggerel verse to his brother he wrote:

*... But if you must know, I've been told in my youth
That Blue is the tint of unchanging TRUTH
And when I look up to the sky so bright
It really would seem that the lesson was right.*

He kept in close touch with the earthly goings on in his home patch as, shown in this extract from a letter, dated April 1831:

'... the fever at Kempsford has been very bad. Mr Huntingdon sent me an account of a plan for emigration — what a good thing it would be if one could get some of the worst in the parish packed off, both for them and for the remaining inhabitants — here there are a lot of idle young men that are always in mischief when any mischief is going on.

He speaks of sending them for 8 pounds, but I should not have thought that possible. My brother seems to like the plan so much that I think he will take it into consideration when he has any leisure to think it well over. You mentioned something of such a plan in one of your letters ... There still seems to be a spirit of discontent among the people

Land Army girls

Two world wars brought the drifters drafted back to the land, but it was the womenfolk who formed the new army defending the home crop and keeping the nation fed. Again, it was the wages anomolies and disparities which caused the unrest. Uncomplaining, the girls from hairdressing salons, city offices and smart dress shops donned the coarse and heavy dungarees and clumsy overcoats, wellies and woollies and Sunday school hats, up before dawn broke to milk cows and feed livestock, manhandle temperamental tractors and hump and haul their way over the farmwork. However, as the lowest paid worker in the country, the land girl did not take kindly to the suggestion that roadmen were to be released from their jobs to help on the land for a shilling an hour when she earned only eight pence.

Gloucestershire had the fourth largest land army force at the end of the first year of the war. Throughout its duration the land girls suffered discrimination over privileges of chocolate and cigarettes afforded their sisters in the serving forces; at the cessation of hostilities they were further affronted by being excluded from demobilization benefits and a service gratuity. A rally at Cheltenham Town Hall was held by land army girls from Southam Priory but, as Joyce Large recalls, 'all we got were our breeches, the sort of blouse schoolgirls do their physical education in, and the heavy old coat only fit for landwork.'

Land force

The labour intensive farming of the mid-nineteenth century absorbed the majority of the work force of a village, and the calendar revolved around the seasonal work; school holidays were fixed by the state of the harvest and haymaking. A cursory glance through the 1851 census shows this:

A land girl's best friend was her cart horse: Mrs Elsie Davey (nee Taylor) with a friend.

Elsie Taylor's land army certificate.

Tea break for the land girls during a visit in the field by their organizer (Elsie Taylor is second from left).

By this personal message I wish to express to you

MISS ELSIE TAYLOR

my appreciation of your loyal and devoted service as a member of the Women's Land Army from 29th June 1944 to 25th November 1949 Your unsparing efforts at a time when the victory of our cause depended on the utmost use of the resources of our land have earned for you the country's gratitude.

Elizabeth R

William Smith of Bibury, farming 733 acres employs 29 labourers

William Trinder (farmer and maltster of 150 acres), employs 6 labourers, 2 boys and 1 woman

Humphrey King, farms 750 acres with a work force of 12 labourers, 7 boys and 6 women

Robert Hinton, employs 6 labourers on his 130 acres.

Oldborough, a hamlet of Blockley, was important enough as a separate farming community to be shown as such in the 1861 census when it had thirty-one people living in eight houses. Within the next decade the population had dwindled to eight and they became incorporated within the township of Blockley.

In 1851 some 1.8 million people, twenty-one per cent of the UK workforce, were engaged in farming; in 1991 this had fallen to around 500,000, less than two per cent of the total workforce.

To be a farmer's boy

The Cotswolds can lay claim to Britain's first agricultural college, and unique as the oldest institution of its kind in the Commonwealth, if not the world. The Royal Agricultural College at Cirencester, founded in 1845, has trained farmers and managers of most of British rural land and many areas of the Commonwealth in its century and a half. Facing the challenges of each changing era, the outstanding contribution made by the incredible Professor Robert Boutflour as Principal was summed up by his own maxim that 'the best way to teach students to farm, is to farm profitably yourself', and this was borne out in just one example of the first herd to average two thousand gallons with three cows giving more than three thousand gallons in a lactation: a far cry from the toddler son and heir learning by following in his father's foot-

steps. Nevertheless, it was to a mixed farm in the Cotswolds, at Park Farm in Fairford, that Prince Erik of Denmark was sent to learn farming. *The Times* reporters trailed the young prince and found him 'sampling the local pleasures of the old hostelry The Bull Hotel' but missed the delight of the locals when he took to playing snooker with tomatoes, using the poker from the open fireplace as his cue.

Lost villages

In a survey carried out in 1981 it was suggested that some 165 sites throughout Gloucestershire indicate former medieval villages. The Black Death decimated a whole generation of agricultural communities in the late fourteenth century, when some four million people died in England of the plague. The depopulation was further accelerated in the new century as avaricious abbeys evicted villagers (such as at Didcot near Dumbleton on the western escarpment) to turn the area into one vast sheepwalk for the booming wool trade. Near Guiting Power, the village of Pinnock is but a name attached to the ghostly humps and hollows of its former being. Henry VIII's itinerant antiquary, Leland, noted in his small handwriting:

'Communely thorough al Glocestershire there is good Plenty of Corn, Pasture and Wood, saving at Coteswold wher the great flokkes of Sheepe be, and yet in sum places ther groweth fair Corn.'

The dour old Radical, William Cobbett, found the Cotswold country 'quite ugly, stone brash' and couldn't ride his rural route fast enough to get to the lush and verdant dairy farmland of the vale below the hill scarp.

Strawberry pickers at Clapton-on-the-Hill in 1934. The village became known as the Strawberry Village, with eight growers who employed pickers from the neighbouring hamlets.

Lost crops:

The tobacco insurrection

Petition:...to practice the same as theyre crops will bee perilled and lost and it will bee to ye ruin of verye manye labourers. May 1652'

The sacking of the monastries by Henry VIII left a disastrous gap in the economy of their dependent towns and villages, especially so was the case at Winchcombe when its great abbey was dissolved. The farming and sheep trade lost its monastic master and could look only to the land for its survival. Unlike its larger neighbour Cheltenham, which turned to malting as an industry, the rural environs had no industrial and commercial facilities to harness. It was John Stratford, whose family roots were in the rich farmland of Farmcote above the also-sacked Hailes Abbey, who introduced the planting of tobacco as a new crop to the Cotswolds. As a London merchant, he no doubt had first-hand knowledge of the potential of 'ye weed called tobacco', for it had already found favour in Elizabeth's court circle from Sir Walter Raleigh's forays into transatlantic territories. It is probably more true to say that he popularized it, as 'ye weed' had been introduced to England by Sir John Hawkins in 1565 during Raleigh's boyhood; it was grown in tentative patches around Westminster soon afterwards and before long appeared at Winchcombe.

The violent disapproval of James I for 'the custom [of smoking ye weed] loathsome to the eye, harmful to the brain, and dangerous to the lungs' brought forth a hefty duty to curtail the importation of tobacco. In his panic to protect his people from the harmful effects of the foreign weed he overlooked a by-then substantial

Tobacco, teasels, orchids and woad for its blue dye have all been grown in their time in the Cotswolds as well as the more conventional crops.

home crop, which, due to his oversight, flourished rapidly — until James was urged to encourage the development of the new English colony of Virginia. To appease the colonists, he turned on his own country and issued a proclamation against the planting of tobacco in England. Heated protracted struggles to protect conflicting interests ensued between the king and his subjects engaged in the trade. It was left to Charles I to issue the first edict to destroy the tobacco crops but the law was evaded or ignored.

'The offenders gather the said tobacco and daily bring it to London by secret ways'. Enforcing the destruction of the crops brought riots in Winchcombe and petitions to Parliament. The Civil War switched the power to Cromwell and the fields were defended by 'a rabble of men and women who called for blood for the tobacco'. Pepys records that in 1667:

'...the Life Guard, which we thought a little while since was sent down into the country about some insurrection, was sent to Winchcombe to spoil the tobacco there, which it seems the people there do plant contrary to law and have always done'.

Records also speak of an audacious bit of treasonous trading by a John Smythe of Winchcombe who actually sent some of the tobacco he grew to Virginia for sale as 'Tobacco English'.

It was finally competition from Virginian growers, both in price and processing, that halted the crop half a century of royal edicts, armed force and parliamentary law had failed to stop. Pepys noted that, following the demise of the tobacco trade in that corner of the Cotswolds, 'Winchcombe is a miserable poor place'.

Teasels

'Teasel and caraway seed are almost alike; it needs a trained man to tell it apart. Crops were grown in the spring and later the plants thinned, standings left and settings transplanted. While the crop was growing, gritting was carried out by running a long spade through the rows and throwing the earth up on either side, followed by spiddling, working the thrown-up earth in among the plants. When grown four to eight feet high they would be cut and lugged by putting on a long pole and dried off in drying sheds. The teasel was ready to cut when the head had finished flowering.'

Henry Riddiford recorded his memories of teasel growing on the Cotswolds as an apprentice to the craft before the end of the last century. The last crop was probably harvested at Alveston in 1900. Once such an important crop for the West of England cloth-making trade, teasels were among the seeds exempted from tolls, while being carried to the grower's land — as evidenced in Turnpike Trust minutes in 1821.

The teasels were graded — into Kings, Queens, Middlens and Buttons — according to size. The main stem bore the King, which was inferior to the Middlens and Queens. Once separated, the different grades were then tied in handfuls to withy sticks in the shape of a half moon, then slipped on to a long split stick and secured with a withy band. Teasel dealers were the agency through which they went before reaching the cloth mills in the Stroud Valley.

Salep for strength

Another short-lived successful crop was the orchid harvest. Its commercial value lay in the roots which made salep, a drink much favoured in Regency coffee houses and thought to be strengthening to those engaged in heavy manual labour. Indian corn, white mustard and coriander were also grown, while the fruits of the caraway were used to flavour Victorian 'seed cake' and its aromatic oil a medicinal ingredient.

Woad

One of the most important dyestuffs used for the fine broadcloth made by Stroudwater clothiers was woad, the blue dye with which the ancient Britons daubed themselves to present a fierce face to invaders. The heyday of the cloth-making period made its mark on the landscape as crops of dyestuffs and teasels superseded arable and pasturelands. About 1770 the Rector of Painswick was in dispute with the dyers over the tithes of woad, which he maintained should be paid to him. Records speak of woad being grown in the area for at least one hundred and fifty years: 'tithes of woad' were traced back to 1615.

The lost art of dew-pond puddling

Dew-ponds, like drocks and ditches, are unmarked monuments to a vanished countryside shaped by the hand of our forefathers. Dew-pond puddlers often travelled around the country practising their old craft of conserving natural water supplies in remote fields on the rolling woldside. Ponds were made by digging a large and fairly shallow hole, covering it thickly with bone-dry straw, then spreading the straw with clay. Stones were packed closely over the clay. Straw is not a heat conductor, so, if built correctly, the ground underneath would not heat up in the sun. The clay remained cool during the day and as night condensation was greater than daily evaporation, the pond gradually filled up. The puddlers got their name from the puddling of the clay into the hole, treading it with their feet. 'We feels it right with our feet,' they said as they judged the correct consistency of the clay. Often, small trees were planted close by in an attempt to attract rainfall, and here and there on very old farmsteads can still be seen the remnants of these ingenious and very effective water supplies, fringed all around with their own self-seeded and naturalized plants.

*Full-scale netting for pike on the Broadwater. The
gamekeeper, village constable and tradesmen all 'had a rod on
the river'. In 1937 Mr C Champion caught 640 pike in three
days — the largest of which had a four-pound trout inside it.*

Riverain crops

'I remember when I was a boy, the watercress cost as much a hamperful as it took a man a week working the beds. Down by the old boathouse you could see old Matty weeding the cressbed as neat as though 'twere his own onion bed. After it was freed of weeds, he had to get rid of the bits of twigs and the flotsam; he used a kind of board for that —like rolling out pastry'.

Bill Monk's memories of the Eastleach watercress beds were as clear as the river which grew what was acknowledged as 'the finest cress in all England'. The secret was not only the purity of the water but that the Leach was never halted by severe frost, and in the season at least a couple of cartloads would leave the small village to be packed into hampers and sent up to London, Birmingham and as far afield as Liverpool, commanding at one time thirteen shillings a hamper.

An otter hunt meets outside the Swan Inn, Southrop, in the 1920s. Farming fish has been a rural industry in the Coln waters since Victorian times; to protect stock, otters were hunted by specially bred hounds. This was banned in the 1970s.

When the May-fly is up

When the mail coach brought the momentous news that the Boer War had ended, there was but a tepid reception in this little Coln Valley market town — as 'the May-fly was up' and, at the time was of more importance.'
Wilts and Gloucestershire Standard.

The crystal clear waters of the Coln are the mecca to which the disciples of old Isaac Walton have been drawn for centuries, armed with the slender rod of their intent, their hats bristling with hooks and tediously tied flies and their patience as endless as their bar-room tales.

'1898 May 6th: As I was fishing I saw a lovely bunch of violets on the opposite side growing out of an old stowle, their rich colouring reflected in the placid

water. Mills says they comes of a Sunday, as though he thinks it right contrary of the fly that it comes up strong on a Sunday. Tis the comicalist thing, he keeps saying — I do believe he would fain see the prejudice against fishing on a Sunday scattered to the four winds. By Jove they're rising.'

Arthur Gibbs stopped his riverside jottings at this point, laying aside his pen for his rod — to be related in detail in meditative reflection on the delight of the Coln trout fishing in his *Cotswold Village*, and the spectacular and ephemeral rise of the May-fly.

The 'rise' is a phenomena of a spiralling cloud of gossamer-winged insects rising from the water, soaring in their hundreds to the heights in a dance of delight of their one and only day of life in the open air. Ian Peters, manager of Bibury Trout Farm, says the purist angler still gets excited by the May-fly; he once had one hatch on his hand, such is the rapidity of the

Bibury Trout Farm in the 1950s. The fish are being fed the old-fashioned way with offal.

metamorphosis of the legendary May-fly which attracts trout and angler alike.

The trout farm is but a little way downstream from Gibbs's manor house grounds through which the Coln wends its winsome way. The swirling and dimpling of the eddies over fallen branches and weed-cushioned stones bring the old England of Bewick's engravings to life. And the Coln is fished for almost its entire length today, more than even in Gibbs's time, but never more so than at Bibury, which he described as 'no prettier village in England than Bibury' — an opinion that was shared by William Morris. Gibbs noted that the higher reaches were, in fact, easier to fish owing to the copious springs feeding the river at Bibury and at intervals downstream.

It is the quality and consistency of temperature of the Bibury Spring coupled with the purity of the water which are the key factors for successful breeding and rearing of trout which have been farmed at Bibury since 1902.

It was a watercress farm in Gibbs's day and some of the older ponds which make up the farm once grew cress. It is an idyllic spot. Linking the low-lying land between the imposing height and buttressed bulk of Arlington Mill and the comfortable length of the old Swan Hotel, where anglers have tied their flies and told their lies for centuries, the lakes and pools and ponds interlace the two parishes of Arlington and Bibury — the farm the central point of what is now one village.

The widest renowned trout farm in Great Britain and the largest of its kind in the country Bibury is haunted by the darting duck and coot and moorhen and the elegant wild swan. Silvery flashes of sleek-skinned trout thrash their way up through the water, darting hither and thither, rolling and plopping to catch some five tons of food a week — with such 'a boiling and a-bubbling' of the water as would have excited old Peregrine right out of the pages of Gibbs's *Cotswold Village.*

The dairy

An aura of timelessness and unhurried activity lingers on in the cool cavernous white-washed dairies of the Cotswold farmsteads. The dairy was a place of scrupulously scrubbed pails and huge shallow pans, slotted ladles, corpse-cold marble slabs and wooden slatted shelves. Tables were bleached and burnished, brushes scouring strong soda water into the very grain. Dimly lit from louvred or zinc-mesh windows, the strange opaque interiors impose their own calm; the noise of pans, churns and china jugs echo the more resonantly because of its bare flagstoned floor. Dairying, be it for butter or cheese making, cannot be hurried and has always been the mistress's domain, with its own delicate branch of superstition and folklore.

Defoe, who had little good to say about Cotswold agriculture, manufactories, commerce or countryside, gave grudging credit to 'the large feeding farms, which we call dairies' and even became excited at some of the farms in the southern hill country when he saw 'great cheeses' in the lofts. Just how great the cheeses were may be judged by a notice offering a reward of twenty pounds for information leading to conviction of an offender who broke open the cheese loft of William Pullin of Charfield in 1795 and stole twenty cheeses. The weight is given as 'two cwt and a half; three of them thick at five to the cwt, one a thick truckle, and all the rest thin, with one marked by the factor'. Green cheeses were new and soft, made in the springtime and much favoured in London.

Double and single Gloucesters are famous, derived from the mahogany-coated Gloucester cow, with a characteristic white stripe along its spine. Cheese is still made in commercial quantities at a Dymock farm, as are other specialities with evocative names from the monastic past. Individual farms sometimes enter the cheese-making field again, and there are several ewe flocks producing soft cheeses and yoghurt.

From the home of the most notable Cotswold sheep, in Mrs Garne's handwritten notebooks, comes a receipt for cream cheese, using cow's milk — normal in the Victorian period. Shakespeare has Perdita going off to milk her ewes, but the fashion waned between the reigns of the two Elizabeths. This receipt must have been written about 1880 (preceding by several pages the Jubilee Pudding for 1887) and is fairly typical of the cheese made by farming wives on the Cotswolds for their own household use.

A dairymaid from Draycott in 1916.

Recipe for A E Garne's Cream Cheese

5 pints of new milk and 1 pint of cream made rather warmer than milk fresh from the cow. Put about 3 dessertspoons of rennet (or according to the strength of the rennet) to turn it and let it stand about 20 minutes or $\frac{1}{2}$ hour.

Put a cloth into a sieve and put the curd into it with a skimmer, let it stand for a few minutes then put a cloth into a hoop and place the curd into it. Fold the cloth over the top and place on it a 3 to 4 lb weight just to press it.

Let it remain for an hour or two, then change into a clean cloth and hoop and let it stay until next morning. It must then have the cloth taken off and be sprinkled with a little salt on both sides. Put a binder of calico round it and leaves on both sides. It must be turned and have fresh leaves and a binder every morning.

The cheese will be ready in about ten days; if put between pewter plates it will be hastened in getting fit.

Strawberry young plant, or raspberry leaves are the best to use. If approved, more cream and less milk may be used.

Cherry curds

The first milk after calving was the cowman's perk, called beestings — pronounced 'bistings'. Simply poured into a pie-dish, the thick creamy milk is topped with a light sprinkling of freshly grated nutmeg and baked in a slow oven until set. It resembles a rich and creamy junket and the pudding is called cherry curds.

Gloucestershire Cotswold fairs: 1830

Bisley
May 4, November 12

Cheltenham
Second Thursday in April,
Holy Thursday, second
Thursday in September,
August 5, December 7 & 18

Chipping Campden
Ash-Wednesday, April 23,
August 5, December 10

Cirencester
Easter Tuesday, July 18,
November 8, Monday before
and after Old Michaelmas
statute, first Monday in
August, September and
October

Dursley
May 6, December 4

Fairford
May 14, November 12

Frampton
April 20

Gloucester
April 5, July 5, September 28,
November 28

Hampton
Trinity Monday, October 29

Iron Acton
April 25, September 13

Lechlade
August 5 and 21, September 9

Marshfield
May 21, October 24

Northleach
Wednesday before May 4,
last Wednesday in May,
first Wednesday in
September,
Wednesday before October 10

Painswick
Whit Tuesday, September 19

Sodbury
May 23, June 24

Stonehouse
May 1, October 11,
November 10

Stow on the Wold
May 12, July 24, October 24

Stroud
May 12, August 21

Tetbury
Ash Wednesday, Wednesday
before and after April 5, July 22

Tockington
May 9, December 6

Winchcombe
last Saturday in March,
May 6, July 23

Wotton Under Edge
September 25

Lechlade May Market

A country workman

Mr and Mrs Rickards from Draycott

Servants and labour

Mop fasteners and servants, obedient and humble

The Mop 'Fasten Penny' was an unwritten contract between Master and the servant he hired on the shake of a hand clasping a penny piece. Later, this became a shilling. The word 'mop' derived from the trade tokens carried by the servants who were putting themselves up for hire at these ancient statute fairs; domestic servants carried a mop, the carter wore whipcord in his hat and the shepherd pinned a lock of wool to his smock.

Tetbury organized their Mop in the year 1863 with a Registry, administered by a Mop Fund to which subscribers paid half-a-crown; non-subscribers had to pay one shilling for each servant hired at the Michaelmas Mop. The resolutions agreed at a meeting at The White Hart in February 1863 were to regulate the hiring and to reward 'a limited number of single servants of subscribers, hired at Tetbury Mop and registered, who shall one week before any subsequent Mop, produce or send to the Committee a certificate of Good Conduct'.

Regulations of servants were imposed by taxes in the previous century as shown in these extracts:

> February the 23rd 1787, Received of William Hicks, Esq. the sum of ten pounds, eighteen shillings and six pence for the House Servants Carriage Horse Tax due at Michael's Mass last.
>
> At the Excise-Office at Wotton under Edge in Gloshire, October 20th 1785 received of John Blag'd Hale, Esq of Alderley – the sum of two pounds four shillings and one penny for two Male Servants retained, or employed by Mrs Smart which he has this Day given in a List, as directed by the Act in that Case provided. Received for One Year ending on the 27th Day of May 1786.
>
> ALL PERSONS ARE TO TAKE NOTICE that they are likewise required by this Act to deliver, or cause to be delivered, within the space of ONE MONTH, after payment of the above-mentioned Duty, a Duplicate of every List, at the OFFICE OF EXCISE, next to each and every House or Place of their Residence, and next to each and every other Place where they shall have retained or employed any Male Servant or Servants, under the penalty of TWENTY POUNDS.

A Servant's Reference of 1737 states:

> This is to certifie to those whom it may concern, that Mary Greenman, who lived with Me is A Labourors Servant. She can go through a great deal of household work very quick, and is not only fit for a housemaid place, but can provide occasion help to ye other Servants. Her parents Live in this place and are very honest good sort of people.
> Augst ye 26th 1737 Eliz Barker

Georgian gentry's servants

The accounts of William Blathwayte give an interesting insight of the colour and grandeur of his servants' livery and the costs of the day as shown in this extract dated 1776, from William Cope.

Making Butlers light coloured cloth coat and scarlet cloth waistcoat and scarlet shag breeches	15s 6d
Silk and twist	3s 6d
Buckram and stays	2s 6d
2 pairs of Linnen pockets	1s 6d
Dimity to line the waistcoat body and sleeves	3s 3d
Glazed linnen to line the coat sleeves	9d
Shammy linings and pockets	3s 9d
Buttons to the suite	3s 0d
One pair of Scarlet silk garters	1s 6d
8 yards Livery Lace at 12d	8s 0d
One silver epaulet	8s 6d
2½ yards livery cloth	£1 12s 6d
1½ yards scarlet cloth	16s 6d
2 yards and ½ scarlet shagg	17s 6d
4 yards and ¾ scarlet shalloon	11s 1d
Making Footman's Livery suite and all materials for same	£5 19s 4d
Making Footman Poole's Livery suite and do	£5 19s 4d

Making Coachman's livery coat and waistcoat and do	£4 10s 0d
Making Groom's livery coat and waistcoat and do	£4 10s 0d
Making Groom's drab surcoat	£2 15s 6d
Making Footman's drab surcoat	£2 15s 6d
Making Butler's drill frock and buff serge waistcoat, lined	£1 9s 6d
Making Under Groom's thicksett frock and scarlet waistcoat	12s 6d
Repairing of black cloth waistcoat	1s 6d
Seating and repairing of black silk breeches, 3 coat buttons and 6 breast buttons	2s 6d

From the accounts it seems that these key servants had a full set of splendid livery, drab surcoats and drill 'frocks' — obviously the latter were for working in as opposed to the splendid scarlet outfits in which the servants danced attendance on their lord and master and added human ornamentation to the mansion at Dyrham Park.

The grace of William and Mary age

The small villages were almost wholly dependent upon the manorial status for their own livelihood. A summary of the establishment of His Grace the Duke of Beaufort at Badminton Park in 1836 gives some idea of both the workforce needed to keep such a ducal seat in the age of grace and the specialist jobs which they performed.

The House employed a House Steward, Butler, Groom of the Chamber, French Cook, 2 Under Butlers, 2 Ushers of the Servants' Hall, 5 Footmen; 1 Steward's Room Boy, 2 Coal Carriers, a Man to attend to the Lamps, and a Man each to attend to Heating the Rooms by Steam and to do the Fire Flues; 2 men to pump the water, 2 House Carpenters and Painter and Gilder, a Brewer, a Maltster and a Baker. 2 'odd men' were employed especially for 'Sundry work', Her Grace and her domain kept busy 1 Housekeeper, 4 Lady's Maids, 1 Seamstress, 4 House Maids, 3 Charwomen, 2 Stillroom Maids, 4 Nurses and Nursery Assistants, 2 Dairy Maids, 4 Laundresses, 4 Washerwomen, 5 women 'in the Kitchen', 1 Clerk of the Kitchen, 1 Butcher and his man and a knife boy. The Stable employed 1 Head Groom, 1 Coachman, a second coachman, 2 Postillions, 3 Pad Grooms, 1 Carriage Washer, 33 Stablemen and helpers. The Kennels of 120 hunting hounds, breeding, pups and pointers kept another 7 men busy; the Garden some 29, including 1 florist and 8 women specifically for the flower beds and pleasure grounds; 14 Men managed the game and park of 1,400 fallow deer and 400 Red at a cost of £70 per week for hay, beans, etc. 14 labourers worked the farm under a Head and Under Bailiff with 16 mules and 3 teams of oxen (4 to a team). A further 28 tradesmen, under a Clerk of the Works, painted, plumbed, glazed, shod, forged, wrought and sawed on the estate.

In service

By the end of the Victorian age it was not only the Big House which had its army of servants; every professional family could boast at least a small regiment, with farmers and traders their own Jack-of-all-trades and Jill-of-all-work. For many girls Service was considered the worthy career, far superior to shop work 'where you're everyone's servant', or nursing which took many decades to shake off its once 'not quite nice for young ladies' image. If she was with a 'good family', the girl was assured of a decent bed and meals, a smart uniform and the opportunity to learn nice ways, handle good china and glass and earn a respected niche for herself. Many sought better standards of living from their own backgrounds when they married. It was not unusual for the mistress of the house to have to give her approval of a match — essential if both were of her household. For the unfortunate ones it was no more than servile sentence.

'I came home from school at 3.30. Mother had the tin bath in front of the kitchen range all ready and I had to get in quick and have my bath, the side nearest the fire was scorching pink on my wet body, the other side all dappled white and blue with goosepimples from the draught through the door. Then into a second hand print frock, a hasty rake through of my hair. My Gran's Sunday and funeral and tea meeting-going hat jammed on top, and a change of knickers and petticoat in a brown paper package was hooked over my hand on its string and we were off. Mother walked with me between the brooks at South Cerney and handed me over to the Cook at the back door. I was just 13 years old and didn't get a half-day off for a month.'

Esther Wheeler's memories of leaving for work half an hour after she left the village school in 1900, having passed Standard IV —the required standard by which eligibility for employment was gauged —are etched into an age so far removed from the present. But conditions did not change a great deal between the wars. Edna Morse's introduction into the Down Stairs world were equally traumatic.

'The Headteacher arranged for my first job and simply recommended me for the post of under parlour maid without asking me whether I would like to do it. My mother, however, insisted on interviewing the lady of the house and thinking she would be suitable for me to work for, agreed that I should go the day after my 14th birthday.

The head housekeeper took over completely. I worked from 6 in the morning until midnight. I was so tired and scared of being up late that I slept on top of the bed fully clothed ready to take her cup of tea in bed dead on 6 o'clock. She confiscated my little bag of apples which I took with me as she said I was five minutes late arriving. She was such a bully. I was not allowed outside the gates of Pope's Court for a whole month. She gave me my month's salary of five shillings and said I was due for a half day off. It was 2 o'clock in the afternoon and she towered over me and

Edwardian afternoon tea.

demanded that I should be back inside at 8 o'clock. It was like being released from prison — and with my first pay packet. I got on my bicycle — which she had chained up for the month — and pedalled off as fast as my legs would carry me down to Lechlade and bought a lovely wooden bowl with an ounce of tobacco for my Pop and a pretty tin full of my Mum's favourite Earl Grey tea. By the time I had cycled home another five miles it was half past three. I was so delighted to buy them a present each out of my first and hard-worked-for wages. I had to cycle back another four miles to get in by 8, and I just collapsed. The doctor insisted I left the job. I had to return my five shillings as he wouldn't let me work out a month's notice; I broke my heart at asking my Mum and Pop to lend me back the money I spent on their presents. I never did see the lady I worked for — everything had to go through the housekeeper.'

Lyfe so shorte — ye crafte so long to learne

Apprenticeships to craft and calling date back to the medieval guilds and changed little in constrictive conditions for centuries. In the eighteenth century many apprenticeships were a combination of elementary education and learning a trade, as at Powells School of Industry in Cirencester:

'Yellow School, Dec 1786:...that the eight eldest boys be at the same time set to the frame for the purpose of learning the trade and that the other four boys be employed to read, write and cast accounts, as also to spin, to double worsted and to seam stockings ...and become bound to the Master as an Apprentice for seven years, and until he shall arrive at the Age of Twenty-one.'

Lady Mico's Apprenticeship Charity at Fairford includes indentures dating from 1703 in which the apprentice was not 'to haunt alehouses, nor play at cards or dice, not to absent himself day nor night

without his master's consent, nor enter into matrimony' for the seven-year term for which he was bound.

'1737: Joseph Boulton apprenticed to Charles Morgan, Gentleman Farmer, till he is 24 years (according to statute) to learn husbandry. The master to provide a good new suit for Holydays and another suit for working days.'

An apprentice to a 'peruke maker' had to take with him 'four new Dowlace shirts, three new pairs of stockings and two of shoes', which the master had to pay for repair and replace all at the end of the term of apprenticeship. Apprentices often ran away and magistrates' warrants were issued for their arrest; there are many cases in the records of masters ill-treating their young apprentices, keeping them short of food and clothing and often beating them.

'1855:(Overseer expenses) Paid expenses for prosecuting Richard Gladwin, Blacksmith of Poulton, for neglecting his apprentice, Thomas Rose — 10 shillings.'

An apprenticeship indenture dated 1898 contracting Frederick Rodman of Sinwell to John Hunt a boot and shoemaker of Wotton under Edge, 1898 states that he 'shall do no damage to his master, nor waste the goods of his said master, shall not haunt taverns nor playhouses, nor enter into matrimony'.

The indenture of John Turner of Cowley, binding to Samuel Gibbons, a broadweaver of Stroud, was even more specific:

'1743:...for the term of eight years will faithfully serve and his Secrets keep. [Then, handwritten within the usual 'he shalt nots'] ...he Shall Not commit Fornication nor contract Matrimony during the term.'

At the end of this term John Turner was, in return for the suppression of his lust for gambling, drink and women, promised a 'full understanding of the mysteries of the craft of broadweaver and double apparel goods for working and one good suit for holydays'.

Buying freedom

A very well written letter from a slave requesting his freedom from bondage to Edward Codrington of Dodington, whose family had estates in the West Indies, offers in return to 'bind myself down to serve you in the farrier's line'. Addressed from Cotton N Work Estate (date indecipherable) the Most Humble and Obedient Servant asks —

'My Dear Master
I have taken the liberty of addressing you on a most particular favour, that is asking your permission to allow me the privilege of purchasing myself and I hope this may not be an offence to you ...I shiver at the attempt of asking the favour from knowing that you have a family which must inherit us here after ... nor shall I shrink from the profession that I now hold ...it is never my intention if I was three times free to give up that name of (CBC)...'

Inheriting the family of servants was obviously not the intention of a Mr Playne, surgeon of Gloucester City, when his servant Elizabeth Richardson was summoned to Court for concealing the birth of an illegitimate female child. A newspaper reports in 1839:

'The prisoner entered Mr Playne's service in October last, and soon afterwards his suspicions were strongly excited that she was in the family way, and he consequently resolved to send her away and obtain another servant ...She said that her shape was the same as it had been for three years and that a medical gentleman in Cirencester had attended her. Mr Playne thought it impossible that he could be deceived ...On the 24th November he saw the prisoner was in labour which she positively denied ... saying nothing of the kind was the matter with her, that she was subject to nervous attacks ...Mr Playne went for a policeman ... [and on his return] discovered the dead body of a child wrapped in a towel. Verdict, not guilty.'

Quarries and mining

Scratch Gloucestershire and find Rome

Civilization far older that that of the Romans rest beneath the humps and hollows of old Cotswold. Throughout all history the earth has been more than scratched, it has been dug into to quarry the fine oolitic limestone with which the Cotsallers raised their homes, the lord's manor and God's church. From the age of pre-recorded history we can still see the chambered long barrows in which Neolithic tribes returned their bones to the earth on which they relied for living. And it is the use of stone, shaped to design of angle and pitch, that has given the Cotswold vernacular its distinctive style and enduring charm; a homogenous whole in tune with the landscape from which it was born.

On foundations of almost a thousand years, the architectural aristocracy of the Cotswolds can be traced to the medieval masons who worked the locally quarried stone for the magnificent parish churches and wool-merchants' halls and houses, tithe barns and manorial estates. It is to this age that the extensive mining of stone became an industry in its own right. Quarrying where the stone lay close to the surface was rather like trenching and tended to arc round the area

selected. This formed a circular pit. The rubble thrown out by the workings raised the sides, which in turn became eroded and the climatization of the limestone-loving creeping herbage completed its own natural form of levelling the landscape. Where the stone lay deepest it was mined.

Mining is not an industry readily associated with the soft rolling hills of the Cotswolds, but south of Minchinhampton the Balls Green stone mines burrow for over two thousand yards in a labyrinth of passages, in which, it is said it is quite possible to get lost. The galleries at the working faces are anything from ten to thirty feet high. They closed at the beginning of the Second World War but, like other stone mines in the region, could well have been used for underground storage and defence purposes. Stone from Balls Green was used in the building of the Houses of Parliament. While the finest building stone from the Cotswolds was used to build the dreaming spired university city of Oxford.

It is the Windrush valley stone which has gone down in the annals as epitomising Cotswold building at its most beautiful. Of rich honey colour, whole vill-

ages of church, manor, cluster of cottages, pigsty and barn are breathtakingly beautiful as they catch the light of a bright setting sun; glowing with the warmth of the summer of centuries, pointed with deep shadow under the overhanging eaves, brushed with shade under delicately drawn dripmoulds, and hung all around with old-fashioned cottage-garden flowers, they are sheer poetry in stone. Under a 'lowery' sky, with low grey clouds pregnant with storm or shower, somehow the buildings stand clear and sharp one from the other, detail drawn in rain-stained roofs and walls as fine as a Dürer etching.

This was the home of the Strong family who worked under the famous shadow of Sir Christopher Wren. From the country quarries at Taynton and nearby Burford the soft golden hued stone went to form the foundation and base of crypt and corridors of St Paul's. Nearer to home and their grass roots, Thomas Strong left money to build a causeway across the water-meadows of the Windrush linking the Barringtons, Little and Great. It is still in use as the road passes the Fox Inn which serves the quartet of villages of the little valley.

The Woodchester pavement incorporates Roman brick in the red tesserae which mingle with the blue, white, and brown colours in the mosaic.

Of strikingly richer hue is the golden stone of Guiting. To come upon the grouping of gatehouse, mansion and church on the sweeping corner in the village of Stanway, with sunshine gilding its every line — dramatic in scale and symmetry — is quite startling as though one has come by chance upon an elaborate stage set with its own proscenium arch. It is this glowing stone which was chosen for the starkly simple style of Prinknash Abbey — a direct contrast to the pearly grey local stone which built its neighbouring village of Painswick.

The fine oolite which caps the north Cotswolds built the lovely old market town of Chipping Campden. Below the limestone is a clay seam along which the waters seep to burst forth again in the hillsides as springs. This is sedge country and the name is reflected in a hill and farm and house hereabouts. Below the clay seam is the inferior oolite which has been mined for centuries.

With only tallow candles to light their dim, dank and drear working day, the men and their faithful horses which dragged the trucks along the underground rail tracks must have longed for the time to come when they could emerge into the fresh clean air of their hillside again. The quarry workings around Campden honeycomb the hills but leave no written route of their form and direction; meanwhile time and clime are reclaiming the spaces left by man in his search for stone.

Of the hundreds of quarries, only a handful remain worked today. The most renowned is Farmington Excavations revealed that at some time in its very long history, Farmington Quarry was mined; today, it is open cast and the whole process — from getting the stone from the ground to carving — is done by hand in the traditional manner. The only machinery in use is for lifting and transporting the stone to the masons' workshop and the giant rotating saws which cut the stone, thus creating smooth flat surfaces.

Bricks have also had their place in the history of Cotswold stone country. One of the oldest and best-known brickfields is at Battledown near Cheltenham. The Romans had their brickfields and one of their earliest in the Cotswolds probably provided material for the world-famous Woodchester Villa. The red tesserae of its incredible Roman mosaic pavement is of brick, the rest being different coloured stone of white, blue and shades of brown. The Woodchester pavement is the largest and most elaborate north of the Alps. It lay beneath the graveyard, preserved by tons of earth which had settled following the collapse of the Roman occupation here, until excavated in the 1790s by Samuel Lysons, who recorded his findings in lovely coloured engravings. For many years the great pavement was unearthed every decade for public viewing, but rapid deterioration has caused re-thinking on how often the 1600-year-old masterpiece ought to be exposed and it has not been unearthed since 1973.

The house paving of yesterday, nearer to our own day, was also of stone — huge stone 'flags', buff and cream and slightly undulating as though still riding the sea bed where the stone was first formed; tiny shells and scraps of fossilized bone and wood embedded in, adding texture and antiquity. Scrubbed clean, the flagstones were then washed over with twice skimmed milk which, when dried on, gave them their distinctive glaze, both attractive and protective on their slightly porous surface.

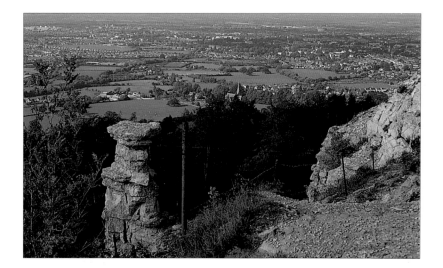

The Devil's Chimney — a unique landmark on the Cotswold escarpment — once the traditional picture of the area seen from railway carriages. The rock pinnacle is a remnant of extensive quarrying at Leckhampton from whence came the stone to build Regency Cheltenham in the vale below.

THE WOOL INDUSTRY

Cotswold sheep

With Cotswold, that great King of Shepherds,
T'whom Sarum's plain gives place,
though famous for her flocks,
Yet hardly does she thythe our Cotswolds' wealthy locks

Michael Drayton, contemporary and fellow countryman of Shakespeare was, like the great bard, a great observer of the native lore and life. Drayton's integrity as a fellow chronicler of the Elizabethan age can be accepted as fact and not merely a poet's fancy phrase. Camden had already singled out the Cotswold breed of sheep as the conspicuous contributor to the wealth of medieval England:

Where Cotswold hillocks famed for weighty sheep
With golden fleeces clothed

The Age of the Golden Fleece, as the period became known, endowed the Cotswolds with the magnificent 'wool' churches. This followed the Golden Age of monasticism, when the great abbeys became as powerful dynasties as the feudal lords, turning the arable, forest and wasteland which had clothed the wolds in the preceding two centuries into vast sheep-walks. The Abbey of Tewkesbury had flocks grazing their way literally across the breadth of the Cotswolds, from west to the Thames watershed in the eastern corner at Lechlade. Equally affluent was the Benedictine Abbey of Gloucester, numbering some ten thousand sheep over its vast estates. The third Lord Berkeley, a famous farmer of his day, maintained on each of his seventy-five manors flocks of no less than three hundred, and often as many as 1,500. To the Cistercians, benevolent landlords renting to smaller farmers as part of their policy of exchanging earlier pious poverty for the dignity and advantages of commercial entrepreneurs, can be traced some measure of their holdings —particularly Hailes Abbey and the awesome scale and simple grandeur of the

Engraving of a Cotswold ram.

Cotswold Lions have thick ruffs and curled lovelocks.

The thick coats of the Cotswold Lions served as winter protection and supported the wealth of medieval England.

tithe barn at Great Coxwell. Dating back to the thirteenth century, the barn was used for sheep shearing at a time when the great tithes had been somewhat depleted after the long winter. Built in Cotswold Gothic style, the tithe barn is generally acknowledged as the finest in all the land.

Cotswold Lions

It was the large-framed Cotswold sheep, with their distinctive curled forelock —which shepherds refer to as the lovelock —bunched between wide-set ears and tumbling down their long aristocratic Roman noses, which carried the wealth of medieval England on their back in heavy long-stapled lustrous and soft curling fleece. A popular jingle of the age was:

In Europe the best wool is English
In England, the best wool is Cotswold.

The long white face, framed by a thick and tightly curled fleece ruff like a lion's mane, gave the sheep the name of Cotswold Lions. Such was the importance of wool to British economy that the Lord Chancellor plumped himself down on a woolsack in Parliament — and has done ever since! The famous Woolsack is, today, stuffed with wool from the four countries of the United Kingdom and still forms the focal point as the seat of the nation's Treasury.

Whether the sheep gave their name to the wolds where they sheltered in their cotes or 'cots', or whether they adopted their name from the hills and rich limestone herbage on which they flourished, is academic. Certainly, the Cotswolds and sheep are synonymous. 'Cotting' sheep was practised by scriptual shepherds: Hezekiah had 'stalls for all manner of beast and cotes for flocks' (2 Chron). Stone-lined shepherds' cots have been found at Ablington, in the Coln Valley and Miserden just below the seven-

hundred-feet contour line, close to an old road leading to Duntisbourne. The latter were excavated some fifty years ago and found to be underground chambers, or at least dug deep enough into the earth as to be considerably sunken and lined with dry stone walling. A crudely built but elaborate system of drainage, also of stone, indicated that these had been designed as dwellings for the shepherds before the wooden hut on wheels was invented.

The Cotswold breed left a rich heritage in its wake, enough to pay the ransom for Richard I after his capture in 1191 and to provide annually thirty thousand sacks of lustrous wool for Edward II's household. Chosen by the King of Portugal for his own cloth of gold, it bore the seal as 'the staple trade of the Kingdom' and rode the storms of political factions, changing fashions, the Industrial Revolution, competition from the Spanish Merino and cheap imports — until the 'agricultural improvers' cross-bred the old breeds to produce superior meat but inferior fleece.

By the turn of the century, the large joints required by big Victorian families were out of favour but foreign wool had ousted the native fleece from the market place.

In 1859 Robert Garne produced a Cotswold sheep for the Christmas Market weighing forty-three stone; one of the legs of mutton weighed fifty-four pounds. Robert Garne founded the Cotswold Sheep Society in 1892 when the breed was nearing extinction. Due entirely to the foresight and tenacity to tradition of Mr Garne, his family and a handful of farmers, the Society has retained interest in the breed and ensured its survival to once again take its place in the top shows in the country, winning many prizes and promoting the Rare Breeds Survival Trust. The Grand Old Master of British Sheepfarming, as old Mr Garne was esteemed in agricultural circles, never exhibited at any show but the Royal from 1848, scooping up the prizes year after year. *The Agricultural Gazette* of 1869

noted that the older Cotswold breeders had discontinued showing at the Royal . . .

The Cotswold breed is now rarely represented according to its merits. The noblest breed in the country is in the hands of a somewhat quiet and homely body of agriculturists — perhaps more averse than most to the quackery and puffery of mere display.

Cotswold shepherds are as noble a breed as the sheep they tend. When Jack Bond died, the last of the old Garne flock shepherds, he was buried with a lock of his beloved Cotswolds laid on his chest, in the manner of the shepherds of old.

Lambs' tails were a shepherd's perk and favourite delicacy. Mrs Evelyn Garne recalled Shep Webb, who minded the famous Garne flock as his father had done before him, enjoying his lambs' tails steamed in a suet crust pudding 'with a hint of onion'.

Language of the hills

Sheep were counted by the score, just as all good country chicken still lay eggs in dozens, not tens! The ancient British sheep counting varies regionally. The Cotswolds way relates closely to the Celtic form.

Yan	one	Yan-a-dick	eleven
Tyan	two	Tyan-a-dick	twelve
Tethera	three	Tethera-a-dick	thirteen
Methera	four	Methera-a-dick	fourteen
Pimp	five	Bumfit	fifteen
Sethera	six	Yan-a-bumfit	sixteen
Pethera	seven	Tyan-a-bumfit	seventeen
Hovera	eight	Tethera-a-bumfit	eighteen
Dovera	nine	Methera-a-bumfit	nineteen
Dick	ten	Gigot	twenty

At twenty a stone was dropped, or put in the pocket, and counting started again.

Arlington Mill, once a corn mill, turned to fulling the cloth hand-woven in the nearby cottages of Arlington Row.

Arlington Row.

Traditions

It was a lucky omen if a new-born lamb was looking at you when first seen.

Sheep bells were passed only from one shepherd to another, never out of 'the calling'.

It was always considered unlucky to count live lambs so they counted the tails as they were cut off. These became the shepherd's perks and were boiled in little cast-iron pots on three legs over an open fire in the sheepfield to remove the wool before the meat was enjoyed in a pie or a pudding.

Page 134
Shep Webb hand-shearing the famous Garne Cotswold sheep — at one time the only surviving flock of this ancient breed.

Woollen cloth industry

*When weavers in their glory stood
And abb and chain were very good.*

Weaving is Cotswold's oldest industry, and the fame of West of England cloth is universal. The art of weaving was known to the ancient civilizations, and the Romans made use of the wool of the large white sheep which they imported to the wolds to improve the smaller native breed from which the distinctive Cotswold sheep evolved.

It is known that a considerable export trade in raw wool was carried out to the continent before the Conquest, but it was not until the reign of Edward III that the skill of clothworking was introduced by Flemish weavers. Induced to bring their mysteries of the craft with them on the promises of exchanging their frugal fare of herring and cheese for English beef and mutton, cooked for them by 'English beauties that the most curious foreigners cannot but commend them', and to escape the religious persecution raging in the Netherlands, a great number of Flemings settled in this country. A further influx of French Hugenots added to 'vast multitudes' of Flemish weavers under the protection of Elizabeth I and 'a great proportion of them settled in Gloucestershire'.

Mills for fulling and dyeing were scattered along the five main rivers of the Cotswolds, alternating their uses over the centuries with milling corn, but it was the steeper hills of the Stroud Valley which gave the power to the mills which were built in the valley bottoms, trapping the water in huge lakes to drive the great waterwheels and provide the vast quantities needed in the many processes.

Bales of raw wool would be bought at one of the marketing towns, taken on packhorse to deliver out to the cottages for cleansing, carding and spinning. Often the cleansing was done by a number of women

Weaving prices in Gloucester in 1834.

Prices for Weaving,
AS PAID BY THE
PRINCIPAL MANUFACTURERS
IN THE
COUNTY OF GLOUCESTER.
MARCH the 4th, 1834.

CASSERENE.

	s.	d.	
Coloured	1	10	per Ell.
White	1	7	ditto

CASSIMERE.

	s.	d.	
Double Milled, ready for the loom		10	per Yard.
Single ditto, ditto	1	0	ditto

FELT OR BROAD CLOTH.

COLOURED.

	s.	d.	
19 hundred	1	9	per Ell.
18 ditto	1	8	ditto
17 ditto	1	7	ditto
16 ditto	1	6	ditto

WHITE.

	s.	d.	
20 hundred	1	6	per Ell.
19 ditto	1	5	ditto
18 ditto	1	4	ditto
17 ditto	1	3	ditto
16 ditto	1	2	ditto

Four Beers to be paid for as a full hundred.

SPANISH AND SUPER STRIPES.

SPANISH.

		s.	d.	
14 hundred			11	per Ell.
14 ditto	and 2 beers		11½	ditto
14 ditto	and 4 ditto	1	0	ditto
15 ditto		1	0	ditto
15 ditto	and 2 beers	1	0½	ditto
15 ditto	and 4 ditto	1	1	ditto

SUPER.

		s.	d.	
11 hundred			9	per Ell.
11 ditto	and 2 beers		9½	ditto
11 ditto	and 4 ditto		10	ditto
12 ditto			10	ditto
12 ditto	and 2 beers		10½	ditto
12 ditto	and 4 ditto		11	ditto

N. B. Nine-pence out of each Shilling is paid to Weavers in the Factory.

☞ No reduction to be made for Reeling, or Temples, or is the Weaver bound to time.

Partridge, Bookseller and Stationer, Nailsworth.

together in a communal yard where they would beat the fleece rather like flailing corn, to rid it of the worst of the tangles and dirt and debris. When the spinning produced a yarn it was warped into a chain and then passed to a master weaver. Whole families were involved in weaving the cloth, and the craft became one of distinction. A number of handloom weavers rose above their humble beginnings and became quite prosperous; others suffered great distress in a system which was so easily exploited by unscrupulous dealers. When the cloth was delivered to the manufacturer and examined, it was then put out to another cottager to be 'burled'; next to a fulling mill, milled and dressed and brought home; then to the dye house to be dyed, washed and racked. The next process was to a shearing house for the raised nap to be shorn close, then home again and pressed. The master clothier then marketed the finished cloth.

The Industrial Revolution turned the world of the cottage industry upside down. Competition from Yorkshire mills and improved transportation meant the Cotswold industry had to change with the times. Introduction of heavy machinery meant building larger mills in an attempt to save what was becoming a decline in a once prosperous trade. A reduction in the handweavers' wages resulted in a three months' strike in 1825 and some five thousand were thrown out of employment. A George Risby appears in a report into the distress caused:

'...Our hours for work are thirteen per day and we work very hard. I earn from 10s to 10s 6d a week. I think my wife get 2s a week, and I do not believe my children get more than 6d a week, as they

Jimmy Pearce, employed by the Playne family: his photograph is still included in their family scrapbooks.

John Mauler, blacksmith at Dunkirk Mill. His family went on strike at Longfords Mill.

cannot earn more now that our abb is spun on bobbins. We are ten in family and after paying house rent of 1s 2d, coal, candles and soap 2s 6d and poor rates of 3d we have only 8s 7d to provide food and raiment ... I am brought so weak that I am not able to work. I and my children are very destitute of clothes. All that we, as Englishmen, want is plenty of labour, and that which sweetens labour. I have four miles a day to walk to my work.'

The intensity of the strike was aimed at the manufacturers, but it was the workers who suffered its effects. Intimidated by organized gangs of rioters who descended on the handloom weavers' cottages and demanded the surrender of their shuttles, the hapless weavers were perforce idle. It was said that the shuttles were hidden in secret places, and some fifty years later some were still not found. Local tradition has it that a number were concealed in church towers around Nailsworth and Stroud. Open defiance turned to violence and at Chalford — where the leaders resorted to the insidious practice of cutting out the beam from the master weaver's loom, setting him astride it and conveying him to the local canal, there to be ducked and humiliated — the military were called in to restore order. 'A troop of horse were engaged for some days in putting down the riot'.

The mill ponds of the factories were the scene of many a ducking of the mill owner as the rioters grew more desperate and vicious, as revealed in the court proceedings of the day.

Photograph on page 138
Dunkirk Mill was one of the most impressive in a valley of beautiful mills.

Three main mills in the valleys near Nailsworth — Longfords Mill, Dunkirk Mill and Egypt Mill — were at one stage all owned by the Playne family.

Egypt Mill, mentioned in the sale notification on the right, was so called because an earlier owner was such a hard task master he was nicknamed 'Pharoah'.

Dunkirk Mills consisted of the principal mill, a cloth warehouse, dye house, drying stoves, drying room, wool warehouse, places for spinning, carding, and weaving, as well as a 8welling house and various cottages.

THE

Valuable Freehold Property

KNOWN AS

DUNKIRK MILLS

NAILSWORTH, GLOUCESTERSHIRE

HITHERTO USED AS A

Manufactory for WEST OF ENGLAND CLOTH

IS OFFERED FOR SALE BY PRIVATE CONTRACT, OR TO LET

It consists of the following Buildings, for the most part stone built and stone tiled :—

PRINCIPAL MILL, 5 stories high, 63 ft. × 34 ft., with Wing 29 ft. × 22 ft.
SPINNING MILL   ditto   62 ft. × 34 ft.
CARDING MILL   ditto   60 ft. × 34 ft.
WEAVING MILL, 4 stories high, 100 ft. × 21 ft., with Wings each 21 ft. × 20 ft.
WILLY MILL   ditto   40 ft. × 35 ft.
WOOL WAREHOUSE   ditto   44 ft. × 28 ft.
DYEHOUSES with ROOMS over   90 ft. × 50 ft.
DRYING STOVES & DYEWARE ROOMS
BLACKSMITH'S & CARPENTER'S SHOPS
Together with a SIDING to the Midland Railway
There are four Overshot Water-wheels and an excellent supply of Water, giving about 45 H.P.
A COMPOUND STEAM ENGINE of 25 H.P.
A HIGH-PRESSURE ditto, of 10 H.P. ; Two BOILERS ; SHAFT 120 ft. high

A CONVENIENT 12-ROOMED DWELLING-HOUSE (at present let)
FOUR COTTAGES AND STABLE

TO LET AT £350 PER ANNUM.   FOR SALE AT £5000

The MACHINERY is offered for sale by Valuation, and consists of 5 Sets of CARDING ENGINES, 40 LOOMS, 6 FULLERS, and all the necessary Machines for Finishing Woollen Cloth.

ALSO

EGYPT MILL AND COTTAGE

NAILSWORTH

Situate close to Railway Station and High Road ; three Floors about 90 ft. × 24 ft. ; two Water-wheels about 20 H.P., suitable for Grist or Shoddy Mill.

TO LET AT £70 PER ANNUM.   FOR SALE AT £800

APPLY TO P. P. & C. PLAYNE, NAILSWORTH

'William Pickford aged 20 charged, with sundry other persons, at Stroud, riotously assembled and committed a violent assault upon William Lambourn, by throwing him into a pond, and at the peril of his life continuing him therein for a long space of time, and with a number of 3,000 and upwards riotously assembled before the woollen factory of Messrs Wyatt and used threats, some bodily harm, to the great terror and annoyance of his Majesty's leige subjects. Committed for 12 calendar months hard labour in Northleach Prison.
Isaac Nutt ...with others, tumultously assembled at Woodchester and violently assaulted and ducked George Teakle. Committed 12 months hard labour.'

At Longfords Mill, one of the earliest users of steam engines, it was the weavers who planned to attack the factory, fearing for their livelihood as machinery took over. The Longfords men turned their production immediately to the creation of a defensive weapon and when the rioters came in force they were met by a counter attack of workers brandishing steel pokers — unique in design and fearsome when wielded — each measuring two feet ten inches and capped by a brass knob fashioned as a man's head.

The wretched conditions of the weavers was large scale as clothiers went bankrupt to compete with the Yorkshire mills, and the labour force was drastically cut to work the machine-powered looms. A Police sergeant at Hampton, reported:

'The weavers are much distressed, they are wretchedly off in bedding; there are many cases where the man and his wife and as many as 7 children have slept on straw laid on the floor with only a torn quilt to cover them ...the children crying for food ... These men have a great dread of going to the Poor

Clothing for 68 persons at £1 10s 8¾d each (including Bibles and Prayer Books given them)	£104 8s 7d
Conveyance from Bisley to Bristol and for provisions on the road and at Bristol	£24 13s 6d
Cash paid for a day's provisions, the first day after their being put on board the Steam packet (*The Leyton*)	£2 0s 0d
Cash paid to Doctor Rogers the Emigrant Surgeon and Inspector, for the expenses of the voyage of George Drake and his wife, and Jonathan Wheeler and his wife (they being above the age allowed to have a free passage) at £15 each	£60 0s 0d
	£191 2s 1d

Houses, and live in constant hope that every day will bring them some work ...the wretched state stints the children in growth, and causes a great deal of sickness ... not one family out of 10 can attend church, in consequence of their ragged condition. [I have] often dropped in at meal times and found them eating potatoes with a bit of flick [fat rendered from the stomach lining of a pig] or suet.'

The calling in of Police officers was to search houses for 'slinge', the name for woollen yarn or woven cloth which some spinners and weavers kept back to sell on to dishonest factors, making up the weight by damping the cloth and all kinds of devious tricks. Cloth was cut out of the tenters on hillsides where they were sited for drying — penalties were harsh, but times were harsher. The decade following the riots was punctuated with poverty and the greatest exodus from the Cotswold valleys and hill villages ever witnessed. Weavers were notoriously inept and apathetic when set to farm work. Some migrated north in search of work in the 'dark satanic mills'; others went westward to the South Wales iron works; a few became railway navvies and vast numbers emigrated, often with parish or Government financial aid as an expedient.

An account by the Overseer of the Poor and a churchwarden illustrates the scale when related to a small village like Bisley, from where in August 1837 some sixty-eight parishioners emigrated to Australia, twenty-six of whom were children under the age of seven years.

Some two years later a report from assistant commissioners surveying the state of the cloth-making industry in the Stroud valleys showed that the first introduction of power looms was in 1836. In the next three years, of forty-three manufacturers listed, eleven employed some one-hundred-and-one power looms between them with a scant work force of eighteen men, seventy-two women and eleven children. Over eight hundred were still working hand looms but by Queen Victoria's Diamond Jubilee, Mr A T Playne was presiding over the centenary celebrations of the Playne family manufactory at Longfords Mill, near Minchinhampton, and stated that the old cottage industry had been completely absorbed in the modern manufacturing processes.

Broad cloth was the backbone of the West of England cloth trade and fame. The purity of the Stroud waters gave striking scarlet for the

36307

Alexander Playne with his wife and two of their ten children on the balcony of the hotel in Montevideo, in South America, where he was buying wool.

The passport issued to Alexander Playne in 1890.

The lake at Longfords Mill.

We, Robert Arthur Talbot Gascoyne Cecil, Marquess of Salisbury, Earl of Salisbury, Viscount Cranborne, Baron Cecil, a Peer of the United Kingdom of Great Britain & Ireland, a Member of Her Britannic Majesty's Most Honourable Privy Council, Knight of the Most Noble Order of the Garter, Her Majesty's Principal Secretary of State for Foreign Affairs, &c &c &c.

Request and require in the Name of Her Majesty all those whom it may concern to allow Alexander Whatley Playne (British subject) proceeding to South America, accompanied by his wife and two children, to pass freely without let or hindrance, and to afford him every assistance and protection of which he may stand in need.

Given at the Foreign Office, London, the 9 day of June 1890

Salisbury

Signature of the Bearer:

Alex. W. Playne

Guardsmen of England; the distinctive Uley blue the superfine uniform of the Navy. The pride with which weavers wove their work into the national fabric moved W S of Nailsworth sometime around the 1880s to compose a folk song.

We are the Jovial Western Boys,
who make broad cloth so mellow,
Did you ever know a Western Boy
that wasn't a jovial fellow?
Though blue we are when at the works,
You'd take us for some smoking Turks,
When work is done, we're ripe for fun
To laugh and chaff with any one.

The Courtier undermines the State, as for the Quacky, he
Your constitution undermines, but to prolong his fee;
The Lawyer undermines your purse,
But none of them can work like us,
For we are bent with full intent
To clothe the frame and give content;
For we are the Jovial Western Boys ...

The 'woaded wool dyed black broad cloth' of which Alexander Playne wrote, clothed and robed the State's dignatories according to a custom which dated back many centuries. *The Daily Mail* reported in 1927 that 4½ yards of the best cloth had again been sent to each of the Lord Chancellor, the Master of the Rolls, the Home Secretary and the Foreign Secretary which, in time-honoured tradition, was a gift from the Livery-men of the City of London. The supply of the cloth was one of their services due in return for the exemption they received from the ancient law passed by King and Parliament which:

'...engaged in reducing the numbers of the retainers of great lords who wore the liveries of their masters'.

Alexander Playne took more than a filial and finan-cial interest in the family business which he joined at the age of eighteen years old in 1871. The Dunkirk Mills at Nailsworth, operating under the partnership of P P & C Playne, was the most impressive of the wool mills in a valley of beautiful mills. Some five storeys housed the main factory, with the dye and scouring houses on site and a glorious lake rather than a mere mill pond. The family also owned two mills at Horsley, Inchbrook Mill, Hope Mill at Brimscombe and Egypt Mills — the latter so named from a previous owner who was dubbed Pharoah as he was such a hard task-master. At their Longfords Mill at Avening the famous superfine broad cloth blazed the name of Playne abroad. Their mills were fully employed day and night for the East India Company for China 'in every conceivable colour in Spanish Stripe'. One contract was for 100,000 pieces of cloth of about fifty yards in length. But it was the dyeing process in which Alex-ander Playne made his own indelible mark.

INVENTION SECRET screamed a headline in *The Daily Mail* in 1927; letters to and articles in *The Times* followed on 'fadeless fabrics secret' which Alexander based on extraction of indigo superseding woad. The formula for dyeing by indigo extraction was the subject of long scientific analyses and lengthier corre-spondence with potentially interested parties, but back home at the mills the receipts were still hand-written in notebooks.

The Playne family could well be described in the local idiom as 'dyed in the cloth' clothiers. Originating from Flemish cloth makers, the de la Plaigne family were brought to England on the advice of Elizabeth I's Privy Council, led by Cecil. Anglicized William Playne, Esquire, quickly made his mark in the right circles and his son, Apollo Playne, had arms granted to him in 1756. The Boscobel tracts show a twelve-year old Thomas Playne in the same house (the Penderels) with Charles II after the Battle of Worcester in 1651. The family had by that time settled close to the Stroud valley waters and were already involved with the

manufacturing carried out in the subsequent cloth industry when some two hundred millfalls were recorded formed on the River Frome and its tributa-ries. To this age the great clothiers' houses of substan-tial size and classic style gave a new architectural dimension to the area. Along with other private persons of standing, many clothiers took advantage of the licence to coin their own pence or halfpence. One Antipas Swineston of Tetbury, Woolman, had a woolbag on the reverse of his coinage; clothiers of Woodchester, Painswick and Winchcombe showed the figure of a man carding wool.

When Thomas Playne died in the early 1800s, his widow Martha, left with eleven children to support, decided to carry on the business. So successful was she that when one of her sons, Peter Playne, died in 1851 he was said to be the richest man in the borough of Stroud. In the parish registers of Rodborough it appears that a Peter Playne was allowed:

'...the liberty to sit in the said (9th) pew and make use of his bassoon, but that no instrument of musick other than a bassoon shall be used there'.

The waxing and waning of the woollen cloth industry, forever at the mercies of that capricious master, fashion, finally waned permanently as the Victorian age drew to a close. Competition from the Yorkshire mills with their cheaper coal and transpor-tation brought to a halt the clack-clack of looms and dull thumping of fulling stocks that decades of civil strife, disastrous fires and economic slumps had not. New industries in old mills sprang up; from an area where they were once counted in many dozens, the Cotswold woollen mills can now be named on the fingers of one hand. Good cloth, specialist cloth, cloth from papal vestments to tennis-ball covering — these are still manufactured in the valleys of the Stroud-water, but the impressive mill buildings, once alive and bustling, are now monuments to a traditional working life relegated to the glorious pages of history.

CRAFTS AND SKILLS

Craftsmen at Bibury
and
Quarrying stone for the masons

Stone masons

The Stone Age is time immemorial in Cotswold country

Bringing stone to life

They could be the fey folk of Beatrix Potter tales; the great men of stone who raised the magnificent Cotswold churches — for they have vanished without name, their work their testimony. Only the diligent searcher will find any trace of their obscure identity, for they 'wrote' their mark in the stone — a signature of angular incised lines, but each has its own identity. These masons' marks are not mystic symbols, they originated as a form of time-sheet from which the master mason would calculate his masons' work. In such a massive undertaking as a church there would have been a great number of workers and it was imperative that the master should be able to identify whose work each section was. It may be that the personal wool-marks of the wool merchants followed the masons', certainly the earliest, said to be of Norman origin, is to be found in the 'wool' church at Northleach.

The seventeenth century brought the family names of Strong and Kempster into focus; from their Cotswold quarries at Burford and Taynton on the eastern edge of the Cotswolds enormous quantities of the creamy coloured stone went by barge from points on the Thames at Lechlade and Radcot Bridge to rebuild London churches after the Great Fire. Thomas Strong laid the first stone of St Paul's Cathedral under the great Christopher Wren and became his major contractor and master mason; Edward, his brother, laid the last stone. Their father, Valentine Strong, is buried in Fairford churchyard under a scroll-topped tomb facing the south door.

Men of stone

A banker mason's name derived from the Teutonic mason who worked at his 'bank' or bench, dressing stone and carving intricate ornamentation, symmetrical pillars, mouldings, cornices and corbels for churches. Today it usually falls to the general builder to repair the fabric of ancient churches but when St Mary's church at Fairford suffered devastation in a mini hurricane in 1970, it was mason Peter Juggins who picked up the scattered pieces from roof and churchyard and started the long lone task of recreating forty-nine pinnacles for the collapsed parapet, and the twin pinnacles of the tower, each weighing some two tons. He became architect, mason and sculptor, seeing the project through from crumbled chaos to artistic achievement. Time and clime have weathered the crisply carved stone at an accelerated rate over due to increased acidity and pollution but the keen eyed will spot Peter Juggins' initials on many a corbel and gargoyle on the string course, and on Tiddles: the famous little statue of the church cat stands sentinel facing the work of this generation's craftsman, close by the tomb of Valentine Strong, the Master Mason of all England.

The memorial is a justified juxtaposition and renews our faith in continuity of an inherent craft of the Cotswold stone country.

A mason whose ancestry in stone can be traced back three centuries, Danny Collett was fourteen when he started his career. After six decades he can still recall the first mouldings he carved and how, 'in indentures', he worked on the university colleges of Queen's, St John's and Trinity. For years he based his work at his mason's yard at Burford bridge, from where the local stone was loaded on to boats to be taken to the cities. The song of centuries rings out as his great bell-shaped applewood mallet, its handle undulated by the grip of three hundred years, strikes the iron head of the keen-edge chisels, as the huge block of stone turns into a fine filigree lace of tracery.

Tiddles: a church cat immortalized in stone.

Stone walls

Cotswold wears her stone like a necklace — a ceremonial chain that gives identity to the land from which it came. Mile upon mile of dry stone walls wind up and over hill and wold, encircling sprawling estates and enclosing churchyard, cottage garden and roadway. Defining boundaries with the oolite stone which lies close to the surface dates back to the Iron Age farmers but the Georgian enclosures brought about the need for solid marking out and most walls that edge field and farm were built then. Quickthorn hedges which grew so readily in richer soils elsewhere did not make the same fast growth in the thinner limestone 'brash' — which Cobbett on his rural rides found 'quite ugly country'. The stone, which he commented on lying so readily exposed in the fields, provided the natural source from which the subsoil rock could be dug to build the walls to enclose them.

The weight, interlocking shapes, and rough texture create natural adhesion in a dry stone wall — a good waller never chops the stone to fit!

Woodchester Mansion is set in a remote valley. Built in the mid 1800s, it brought together the expertise of many stone masons. The stonework is wonderfully carved and detailed, with ornate ceilings, mullioned windows, massive fireplaces, gargoyles and stone vaulting and tracery — all resplendent in a house that, mysteriously, has remained empty ever since it was built.

Stone roofs

The stone was spread out in the frost to help it split along the natural divisions. Slatters erected shelters of stone or straw-covered hurdles and camped out, trimming the slates with a slat hammer. Peg holes were made at the thinnest point on the topmost edge, ready for the slates to be secured with wooden pegs and set into sweeps or valleys. The tile size graduated from small ones at the top of the roof to sometimes quite massive ones at the base.

Stone tiled roof at Woodchester Mansion.

Making stone tiles at Cerney fields.

Homer describes the art of building mortarless walls and some claim that the Romans introduced these to the Cotswolds but dry stone walling was practised by the neolithic settlers.

Stone slates

Quarrying was usually carried out in the early autumn; the slabs of stone were covered with turf sods to retain the moisture and keep them 'green'. When the first frosts arrived the tiles were uncovered and laid flat on the ground to exclude air. The frost expanded the 'bed' of the tile. Splitting it into layers was then made easier by carefully tapping round the edges until the vulnerable point was reached. The tiles then had to be squared off and a peg hole pierced at the top, from which the tile hung on the roof rafters. When graded for size, the tiles were stacked — a skill in itself for they had to lean against each other so as to be supported — otherwise the whole lot would collapse like a pack of cards and smash. Those six to eighteen inches long were stacked to four hundred; nineteen- to thirty-inch tiles were stacked at the ends to twenty-five. This constituted five hundred, enough to roof an area of ten square feet. Like the baker's dozen in reverse, the larger tiles counted as twenty-five to the hundred, instead of 'thirteen to the dozen'.

The spirit of the stone and the Jubilee Boy

It is the local stone that creates the enduring beauty of the Cotswolds where buildings harmonize with the landscape in whose womb they were conceived as great blocks of oolite limestone. A thousand years of quarrying scars the eastern edge where the inferior oolite of meets the great oolite of Oxfordshire. From the latter comes the fine-grained freestone, cut quite easily when freshly quarried and hardening when exposed to the elements, making it ideal for carving and ornate work. The Norman masons drew their stone from the local quarries and masons have been using it ever since — to raise the dreaming spires of Oxford and the splendour of Blenheim Palace. Some two thousand tons of it floated down the Thames on barges to build Windsor Castle, and later to rebuild the capital's fire-destroyed churches.

The stone taken from the heart of Cotswold country stands today — catching the light it radiates a myriad of colours from gold to grey, cream to bronze with a dozen hues between — the very spirit of the earth raised and shaped by generations of men with stonedust on their hands and poetry in their hearts.

'There was very little smocking on our masons' smocks, 'cos the dust got lodged in the little dents, that's why 'twas I reckon'

George Swinford, born in the Golden Jubilee year of Queen Victoria, celebrated his centenary by publishing his first book, *The Jubilee Boy* and a crystal clear memory still recalls the past:

'I remember when the old lady passed away — I was at work moving the stones from the old house called Paul's Castle and we heard the church bell tolling. "Ah," I said to my mate, "England's old mother's gone", and we took off our hats and stood quiet for a good minute'.

George Swinford's joy was converting the coach-house for Gimson at Sapperton and, later, as mason for him at Kelmscott Manor for William Morris's daughter. George recalled the wages in 1912 were, '6½d an hour for tradesmen — that was mason's rates; and 4d an hour for labourers, so i was earning £1 14s 8d for a 64-hour week, before any deductions.'

Sizing the stone slates

At one time the measurements of stone tiles was a trade secret: each region had its own set of quaint calculations; all were measured on a wippet stick, marked in Roman numerals — easier to cut than Arabic ones. A nail at the top serves as a peg on which to hang the tile and the length is read off in a language known only to the 'slatter' of that area.

On the right are tile names from three areas, reading from the roof ridge down.

Stow on the Wold	Bourton-on-the-Water	Tetbury
short cocks	short cocks	farewells
long cocks	middle cocks	wippets
short cuttings	long cocks	chivelers
long cuttings	short cuttings	long chivelers
movities	long cuttings	guardians
short becks	maverday	long guardians
mid-becks	short backs	cuttings
long becks	middle backs	long cuttings
short bachelors	long backs	wivets
long bachelors	short bachelors	long wivets
short nines	short nines	spots
long nines	long nines	long spots
short vibbots	short wivetts	nines
long vibbots	short elevens	long nines
short elevens	long elevens	short tens
long elevens	short twelves	(increasing by longs and shorts to seventeen)
short twelves	long twelves	
long twelves	short thirteens	
(increasing shorts and longs to seventeens)	long thirteens	
	(increasing to sixteens)	

Master craftsmen

The thatcher

*'. . . or doest come from whur they thatches thur pigsties
with pancakes?'*

This ancient line in the Cotswold's Mummers
Play has an element of feasibility in it;
'thatch' originating from the Saxon word
thaec, meant roofing. All manner of material was used
— reed, straw, bracken, wood shavings, turves or
heather, whatever came to hand for church, cottage,
haystack, manor or pigsty alike, as evidenced in excavated neolithic sites. In Cotswold stone country, straw
thatch gradually became displaced by the native stone
slats (tiles), and only the humbler dwellings sheltered
under a straw or reed thatched roof.

Before the thatcher can begin his task, he must
strip off the ols thatch before he can build up a new
one. Roof rafters have to be treated for worm or decay,
sometimes having to be renewed entirely. Only then
can the thatcher estimate the amount of long straw,
which is the type used in the Cotswolds, which he will
need for the task. A modest-sized cottage will take
some three tons to re-roof.

Combed wheat straw, to give it its proper name, is
still being grown by a limited number of farmers to
meet the demand. The crop has to be harvested in
traditional manner and, indeed, grown without artificial fertilizer which, being mainly salt-based, weakens

the straw because of its water-drawing properties.
The crop is then harvested by a binder when the straw
is at its peak, before the wheat ripens, then stooked to
dry naturally. The flag — the leaf of the straw which
grows down it — is then combed by a special attach-
ment to a threshing machine.

The craft of thatching is physically exacting: each
straw has to be carried on to the roof. Apart from the
initial transporting of the load of straw to the site,
there is not a modicum of mechanization involved. It is

totally labour-intensive and most thatchers prefer to
work alone, so total commitment is necessary. A fair
amount of preparation work is involved in the
'yealming'; this is grading and gathering the straw
into manageable 'dollies'. The only bundles to be laid
horizontally are those which form the ridge roll,
giving pitch to the roof and a solid foundation into
which the pegs can bite.

Laid vertically from eaves to ridge in widths of two
to three feet, the thatcher 'courses' along the roof
working from right to left — having to move the ladder
as he goes. Each bundle of straw is laid separately.
After being carefully positioned it must lie at the
correct angle. The base end is stroked and coaxed,
tapped and dressed by knocking the hollow ends with
a leggat — a square board on a handle. Then the bundle
is secured with hazel pegs. Some six thousand will be
used to pin down the thatch on a medium-sized
cottage. Finally, the eave edge will be sheared off
neatly and the ridge top finished with an ornamental
ridge; the pattern will be the hallmark of the
craftsman who thatched the roof.

Thatched property owners are better protected
today than in all history. There is a comprehensive
advisory service and more enlightened insurance
brokers, but the staunchest support comes from the
formation of the National Society of Master
Thatchers, formed and run by the craftsmen who
jealously uphold their reputation and maintain their
prestigious and ancient skills.

*David White, re-roofing the smallest Post Office in the
Cotswolds, continues the family tradition of thatching alone.
Keeping the ears on the 'dollie' gives added thickness but they
have to come off for the difficult curves of a swept valley. Each
'dollie' has to be carried on to the roof. Leather knee pads give
protection and afford a grip on the slippery straw.*

The wheelwright

There is an old Cotswold saying that a wheelwright can do any kind of cabinet-making, but a cabinet-maker would be hard put to make a wheel.

Once to be found in every village, the wheelwright's shop was as active as the blacksmith's forge — they kept the community together with their skills: many wheelwrights were also undertakers and the old oil lamps would be burning half the night when there was a coffin to be made amid the miscellany of the parish furnishings, implements and vehicles. The wheelwright's diversity in timber would take him up to the church's vaulted roof where he would perform feats akin to the old shipwright's, or down on the farm to repair a wagon or shepherd's hut. Little wonder that the term for apprenticeship was seven years. The dished wheel is a particularly English design, and the narrower tread peculiar to the Cotswolds, evolved to cope with the lighter soil of the region. At the peak of the farm-wagon era, around the 1870s, wheels were increasingly shod with heated iron hoops; as the metal contracted, it gripped the wheel in a self-sealed bond.

'Elm for the nave, oak for the spokes and ash for the felloes.'

A magnificent piece of workmanship, the harvest wagon could be called engineering in wood. Every curve of the body was designed to take the stress imposed on it by the regional terrain.

Chamfering, decorative as it appears, was not meant as ornamentation but to pare away all surplus timber to lighten the total weight. The wagon with its load was heavy enough for the noble horses to draw from field to barn, and the wheelwrights had this in mind as they refined the curves into sweeps or double curves according to the part of the body and wheels which needed support.

The harvest wagon was the most versatile vehicle of the community — it took the chapel and church outings on happy picnics, headed a funeral cortege of the farmer, was a mobile stage for the local outdoor performances and, as here at Leighterton in the Thirties, provided an excellent grandstand at the Point to Point.

Through the glass brightly

As old as the hills, glass making was discovered by accident in the ancient East. Pliny the Elder told of Phoenicians finding blobs of translucent glass on the beach where sailors had set up their cooking pot, propped on a form of soda. The silica, a mineral element of sand, flint and quartz, when mixed with soda or potash and subjected to intense heat, becomes a molten material, so flexible that it can be stretched and rolled into sheets, or twisted and blown into bubbles so light they float in the air. The art of glass making was practised by the Romans but in 647 the Venerable Bede writes that the craft of glazing was unknown in this country at that time. By the twelfth and thirteenth centuries England was leading the field, and the medieval wool merchants glazed and glorified the parish churches they built on the wealth they amassed from the vast sheepwalks in which they traded fleece for fortune.

Today Colin Stokes puts life into the light of his stained glasswork. As an architectural element it has hardly ever been dissociated from its ecclesiastical foundations, except for a flush of fashionable features in Victorian villas on lofty landings and distinguishing front doors of doctors and dentists. Snails, not saints; birds and bees and butterflies; fungi, feathers and whiskery barley; the fruit, flowers and nuts of hedgerows are this artist's style — a cornucopia of Cotswold caught in an explosion of colour.

The Cotswolds is particularly well endowed with beautiful church windows — from the massive east window of Gloucester Cathedral to small private chapels, and a great cluster of 'wool churches', such as found at Chipping Campden, Fairford, Lechlade, and Northleach. Of their artists little is known and their authorship is attributed by different authorities to an anonymous body of English and Flemish painters, so it is with local pride that great windows from the famous Payne studios are pointed out: — first, Henry Payne and then his son Edward.

The stages from concept to completion of a piece of stained glasswork have changed not a whit since the medieval artists gave the 'poor man's bible' a visual interpretation. Once the design has been agreed upon, a working cartoon of the correct size and shape is drawn up. This indicates the leading lines which form an integral part of the design as well as holding the individual pieces of glass together. Although some segments of the design will be painted, stained glass is the technique by which the metal oxide paint, when heated, fuses to become part of the glass itself. Silver salts on the back of the glass are a stain rather than paint and are transparent.

A duplicate cartoon is made and each segment is numbered. It must be exact as this is the template to which the coloured glass is cut — now with a diamond cutter in a pen-like tool. Earlier artists had to put oil on the surface of the glass, apply a red-hot iron to the lines and cut with a grozing iron. The grozing iron is still used, in fact. Resembling a huge pair of pincers, it is essential for the smaller pieces of glass and for nibbling away at an edge to obtain the precise measurement required.

It is at this stage that the actual painting or etching, badgering with a brush, stippling, acid etching, silverstaining and engraving are done. A dandelion seedhead can comprise several hundred individual strokes and scratches made with a finely sharpened farrier's nail to capture the gossamer frailty before firing — perhaps several times. After firing, all the pieces are laid on to the cartoon in number order ready for leading up. This is a highly complex task, building and moulding and jointing and tallowing the pieces together into the H-shaped lead leaves. Finally, a mix of linseed oil, putty and soot is rubbed over both sides to seal the glass securely and bring up a sparkling brilliance to the splendid great mosaic.

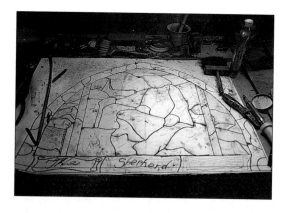

*Working cartoon of
the design.*

The Cotswold Shepherd *by Colin Stokes, showing Tetbury church in the background and illustrating the old Cotswold shepherd's maxim about moving the sheep to new pasture every week. The artist actually keeps his own flock of sheep and builds the stone wall cots around their fields within the sound of Tetbury church bells.*

1914: Young Herbie Hayes proudly stands next to his father who made the horse's collar on his shoulder. Mr Cooper, saddler, stands on the right. They also made and sold dry-fly fishing tackle.

A jockey, armed with his sadddle, waits in the paddock at Leighterton Point to Point in the 1930s.

The saddler

'The problem today is to make tough leather from tender hides.'

Changes in agricultural methods mean that hides are less fibrous and more gelatinous than in the days when cattle were allowed to grow older on the hoof and toughen as they weathered. The saddler has now to shop around; the discerning will find the few that hand-stain and curry so that each pair of butts is treated in a selective manner to ensure the leather is dressed throughout the fibres.

The old leather trades were mainly sited at the termini of the drovers' roads when the medieval custom was to slaughter beasts before winter. Large-scale markets concentrated cattle into centres where an adequate water supply enabled manufacturers of by-products to be established. Small-scale tanneries — usually tucked away in a back lane of the village or town because of the obnoxious smell emiting — coped with local demand for whipthong and lacing, beaverskin hats, gloves and shoes. Leather dressing as an important industry can be traced back to the thirteenth century at Oxford and Gloucester — the two extreme boundaries east to west across the Cotswolds. Saddlers and harness-makers were much more locally established by Tudor times and when Elizabeth I made her visit to Burford it was already famous for its saddle-making. The English saddle was by then considered the best in all Europe. The frequent visits of Charles II with his 'pretty, witty Nell' to the then-famous Burford Races and equally famed Bibury Races, made the south-eastern corner of the Cotswolds a mecca for rich and rabble alike; all of whom had to travel by horse.

It was not until the complete subjugation of the horse was harnessed by saddle, stirrup and bit that full control of rider over horse was achieved. The precarious perches upon which early horsemen cantered so recklessly through history into battle and the chase, varied little from a form of stuffed pad attached by a girth until the time of the Norman Conquest. The Romans seemed to totally disregard the need for weight to be distributed each side of the horse's spine; the womenfolk who jolted across the Cotswolds did so in even more perilous position — for their seat was little more than a cushion secured by a girth strap. The earliest surviving example of the 'tree', which allows clearance of the horse's spine to transfer the weight of the rider to its muscular sides, is the saddle tree of Henry V, which has been in Westminster Abbey since his funeral in 1422.

Tree-making, a separate craft from saddlery, creates the frame upon which the saddler shapes the seat for the rider whilst protecting the horse's spine. Creating a bond between horse and rider is the criterion upon which bespoke saddlers work — such as John Hayes, the third generation of the famed Cirencester firm of saddlers. The leather John uses is natural cow hide, traditionally cured, tanned and stained. The thickest and prime part of the hide is from the back of the cow and this is used on the skirts and flaps which take the greatest wear and strain. Hand-stitching in the time-honoured way, using two needles — one on top and the other underneath filled with beeswaxed thread — gives added durability to all strain-bearing sections. Although some machinery is creeping into the workshops, most saddlery and

harness work is still painstakingly hand-stitched. 'The sturdy sewing machine comes in useful for repairing the village hall piano cover, though,' John Hayes laughs. One old saddler maintained that the notice on the workshop should read 'Saddler, Harness maker and what not beside'. The 'what-nots-beside' can be anything from a boot for an elephant with a sprained ankle to making a seat for a vintage motorcycle or finely laced and thonged sheaths for the springs of a vintage Rolls Royce. And adapting saddles for disabled riders, or for camels, are all part of the variety within the craft. Despite fierce competition from cheaper imports, saddlery still exists as one of the Cotswolds' most enduring crafts.

The glover

Woodstock glovers are the last of a line of craftsmen, centred in the Oxfordshire Cotswolds since around Saxon times, who were 'brought up on shears'. It is generally acknowledged that the key craftsman in the gloving industry is the cutter, and the fortune or fall of a company can literally be in his hands. The last of the Woodstock glovers is still using shears, huge blades finely sprung like sheep shears, to cut out the shapes from which the gloves would be made up by the gloveresses — outworkers who make up sixty per cent of the work force. Scissors for cutting are favoured in other regions, so it is a real link with the past that Woodstock maintains in its famous craft.

At one time the leather was completely home-grown; the Cotswolds was an almost unending source of sheepskins and the once large Wychwood Forest, under whose receding shadow Woodstock lies, was abundant with deer. Tanneries were kept busy at Burford, Witney and Chipping Norton to supply the gloving industry which flourished alongside the wool trade in its heyday and lasted for three centuries until the decline at the beginning of this one.

Elizabeth I, a trend-setter of her day, gave the glove a fashionable status. The heavily braided and gold silk embroidered gloves presented to her on her visit to Oxford in 1566 were made at Woodstock and are still in the Ashmolean Museum. Royal hands have been gloved by Woodstock glovers ever since. In the leather-scented workshop is a photograph of our present queen being presented with a pair and the Princess of Wales was similarly honoured. It is a continuation of a long custom that important visitors to Oxford, the city of 'dreaming spires', as well as circuit judges at the beginning of each Assize, are given Woodstock gloves.

After the Industrial Revolution centralized the manufacture of gloves, only sixteen traditional glovers companies remained in the whole of Oxford shire by 1921; eight of these were at Woodstock and four at Charlbury, both within the confines of the Cotswolds. Now only one remains but it is a craft which still lends itself to a cottage industry work force.

Once the skin has been 'straked' — this is a stretching process that evens out the tension and texture — the 'tranks', the main shape of the hand, and the 'fourchettes', between the fingers and thumb pieces, are cut. The tranks are then slit after the raw edges of the skin have been buffed with a 'spudnol' to prevent their fraying.

The batches of gloves are delivered to a team of gloveresses, many of whom learnt their skills from their mothers and grandmothers. The older ones still recall their early days when the payment was 1s 6d ($7\frac{1}{2}$p) for hand-stitching a dozen pairs. The glovers of Woodstock still enjoy the challenge of making a copy of a favourite glove, or designing a two- or three-fingered one for a disabled hand, or a batch of left-handed ones for golfers or a special order for West Indies cricketers and someone will recall their craftsman ancestor who gloved the great batting hands of the legendary W G Grace.

Smiths black and white

> *. . . sitting by the anvil,*
> *And considering the iron work,*
> *The vapour of the fire wasted his flesh,*
> *And he fighteth with the heat of the furnace;*
> *The noise of the hammer and anvil is ever in his ears,*
> *And his eyes look still upon the pattern*
> *of the thing that he maketh;*
> *He setteth his mind to finish his work,*
> *And watcheth to polish it perfectly.*

Since Old Testament times, the blacksmith has inspired writers and the ringing of hammer on anvil is as much a part of the country sounds as birdsong in hedgerows or church bells across a meadow. He is now a rarity but his smithy is still a magical place locked in folklore: the flames from the furnace lick hungrily at the black coals, devouring smoky shapes drawn from deep shadows in cavernous depths where the smith works as the uncrowned king of craftsmen.

For centuries he ruled supreme, forging a long link with the past; his predecessors in the Cotswolds, the mysterious Dobuni, left evidence of their skill in metalwork long before the Romans came. In church and manor, field and farm, cottage and cattleshed, the smith's work is to be seen. Scarcely another trade could be carried out without the tools he forged.

The strength of the blacksmith is legendary; lifting a three-hundredweight anvil up in his hands is part of the job; no wonder every village welcomed the blacksmith into their Home Guard platoon. His was the strength needed to hump unwieldy artillery around and his was the skill essential to make the artillery go when it wouldn't.

The blacksmith at Poulton commemorated Queen Victoria's Diamond Jubilee by building two pillars from over 5,600 horseshoes which weigh 4½ tons. Topped by Union Jack flags and joined by a rail bearing Benjamin Carpenter's initials, this landmark indicates a huge volume of work, being made entirely from cast shoes that he and his father had replaced.

'If old Hitler knew just how dependent the aircraft industry was on the village blacksmith, he'd have bombed the lot of us. I've know when I worked all through the night to get a job done for a ship lying a hundred miles away. When I first started we repaired a lot of irons for legs of men injured in the Great War. I even made a wooden leg for one of the chaps. Can you see a carpenter shoeing a horse or bending a wagon wheel.'

James Rathbone, three times champion blacksmith and awarded the MBE, recalls his apprenticeship during Edwardian days and how from the age of thirteen he worked for two years for nothing other than the privilege of learning the time-honoured skill.

> 'Those were the days when you had to turn up in spotless white corduroys and clean boots, polish the anvil, watch your language and saw the wood properly and cheerfully. It was a long time before you were allowed to touch the fire; it's an unwritten law that you never touch another man's fire.'

In time, James Rathbone and his sons would wrought over a ton of iron in one construction, making 1,500 feet of ironwork into gates at Ascot's Royal Enclosure.

Like the lame Vulcan, and many of his calling, Charlie Bartlett fron Coln St Aldwyns is a blacksmith who carries injuries lightly. He lost an eye while shoeing the Army's horses and high-kicking mules. It can be a hazardous profession in many ways. 'Next to the Inland Revenue officer, the smith is probably the most cheated individual,' one smith remarked. He had sent his wife to evening classes to learn about metalwork as he was desperate for help. She discovered the class was full of young farmers undertaking work which should have gone to the local blacksmith but with government grants, they could set up an unregistered workshop and cobble together repairs with welding equipment and blacksmithing of a sort. But it is the 'barnyard farrier' pirate which really upsets the blacksmith; the one who thinks he can shoe his own horse and subjects it to unnecessary pain as it hobbles around with an altered leg action. The passing of the Farriers (Registration) Act has made it illegal for shoeing to be carried out other than by a competent farrier.

'Preserving of horses' was one of the duties of the Royal Charter granted by Charles II to the Worshipful Company of Farriers, whose guild dates back to 1356.

The farrier, or shoe-smith, has become largely divorced from the blacksmith; he is still a worker in metal but specializes in the profession of shoeing. The most significant change is that the farrier now, generally, takes the forge and anvil to the horse, instead of the horse coming to the smithy. Most shoes today are factory made, cutting down the time the farrier spends at his home forge. A portable forge, compact enough to fit into the back of a van, can be taken to stable or field to the horse.

The horseshoe, with only minor modification, has changed little in design since the Celts introduced the metal rim-type shoe nailed on to the hoof. The invading Romans shod their steeds with much clumsier hippo sandals, metal plates tied on to the hoof with leather thongs like the ones on their own shoes

Depending on how much road work the horse gets, it usually grows enough new hoof — of horny substance like human nails, growing at an average of an inch a month — to warrant a visit from the farrier every six weeks. Often this entails removing the shoes, paring the hooves down and refitting the shoes. The Cotswolds is studded with hunting, riding and polo stables and different horses require the farrier's skill to suit their needs. I watched Mike McCormick, at work on a polo pony. The singeing horn and clouds of

Craftsmen and blacksmiths of Wotton-under-Edge turned their skills to the defence of the realm in war-time, making road blocks from tree trunks and cartwheels.

*Right
The old blacksmith's shop at Coln St Aldwyns in 1900.*

acrid smoke threatened to dispel the romance of a village farriery.

> A good blacksmith made the shoe to fit the hoof, not the hoof to fit the shoe.
> 'He *never* threw anything away. He *never* made any money. You'd *never* see a rich blacksmith.'
> Different heats had vivid names: black heat, snowball, slipper and sweating.

Mike McCormick tapped the front left leg and the horse raised it and bent it at the knee, well used to the procedure. Straddling it comfortably and grasping it firmly between his knees through the traditional split-

front hide apron, Mike made a few deft pulls with enormous pincers — reminiscent of days when the blacksmith would remove aching teeth under the village tree. The nails were out and the shoe removed. While the hoof was cleaned and pared level the new shoe was heating on the portable forge. When cherry-hot — glowing red and transparent at the edges — Mike removed it with long tongs. After being plunged into a bucket of water to cool off, the shoe is matched to the hoof and any metal residue tapped off. Often it must be returned to the forge, reheated and reshaped on the anvil before a perfect fit is made. Then, and only then, is it nailed on with the curiously designed horseshoe nails, tapering from a flat head and curving slightly at the tip to follow the contours of the hoof. Driven in at an angle, the nail tip protrudes through the outer hoof and is clenched back with the claw of the hammer to secure the shoe. There is only a narrow band of hoof to which the shoe can be nailed, for between that and the frog (the fleshy part) is sensitive laminae — a vulnerable nerve membrane which, if damaged, can maim the animal permanently.

Shoes and nails forged by the blacksmith are still associated with magic and luck, and old ones sought as talismans. Many a pub is called the Three Horseshoes and brides are presented with beribboned horseshoes. The Filkins Folk Museum has a fine collection of shoes from mules to highwaymen's — made round by the cunning of the smith, probably at the point of a blunderbuss, so that the pursuing posse could not tell from the hoofprints whither they had gone.

Ironworkers and tinkers

The ornamental iron-worker mainly developed from the diverse skills of the blacksmith who turned his hand to shape everything — church door handles, locks, keys, ploughs, shepherds' crooks, clocks, chimney-pot ratchets, fire dogs and fenders. Apprentices learned to coax curls out of rigid rods, to planish pots and candle holders, to make wind dials and bedheads from many metals. The now extinct tinsman used to fashion pots and pans and tin tubs, carrying them strung around his person when he took to the road as the once-upon-a-time figure of the tinker.

The whitesmith

While blacksmiths worked mainly with iron, whitesmiths wrought their skill with precious metals such as silver. Stuart silver was initially regarded as monetary reserve to pay war expenses and little ornamentation was necessary on plate destined for the melting pot to eke out the next royal budget. Cromwell destroyed it through sheer pique and prejudice but the Restoration saw a revival of the arts and crafts and silversmiths were patronised in the lavish lifestyle which Charles II enjoyed. Among the gifts he bestowed on Nell Gwyn was a silver bed!

When guilds inspired by the William Morris doctrines formed at the turn of the century — aiming to recapture the ethos of the medieval age when craftsmanship was worthy of its material — designer and smith were reunited. C R Ashbee brought his Guild and School of Handicraft from London to Chipping Campden during this revivalistic period. When the Guild broke up in 1908, George Hart, one of the London silversmiths, took over the old silk mill and established a family business which has continued ever since. And today David Hart dons Pickwickian watchmaker's spectacles to engrave silver in the Dickensian workshop. The solid wooden bench is hung around with deep pouches to catch the precious silver filings that can be reclaimed as raw material. In the old days the apprentices had to change their clothes as they entered and left so they could not sell the silver dust and filings caught on the cloth. A hefty hunk of an ancient tree trunk serves the same purpose as when it was hewn; its surface has been hollowed by generations of Harts hammering flat sheets of silver to get it 'blocked down'. Hammers of all shapes and sizes are the smith's main tools. The silver is 'raised' into shape by hammering it on a head held in a vice; the hammer marks are then erased by 'planishing' — squashing the metal between tool and hammer to smooth it.

OUT AND ABOUT

Arthur Davis, village blacksmith at Bisley and champion cyclist. He manufactured his own bicycle gears before these were generally thought of.

Posed for the cameraman — one hopes, both for the sake of the single horse and for those precariously perched passengers!

Charles and Anne Gosling, dressed quite formally for a Sunday afternoon spin on their bicycles in 1898.

A tricycle made for two.

Index

Acknowledgements

Photographs and illustrations

The publishers would like to thank
the photographers and the owners of
photographs and illustrations for their
kind permission for these to be
reproduced in this book.

Atkyns *History of Gloucestershire 1768*
(David Playne collection) 10

Champion, Mike 19, *bottom*,
20 and 24 *top* (Phil Griffiths
Collection), 64 *right* and 87 *three
photographs* (courtesy of Mildred
Kent)

Christie, Harold 32 (Pat Christie)

Christie, Patrick 118

Cole, Eric 17 *bottom*, 109, 135 *top*

Cotswold Countryside Collection,
Northleach, Photographic Collection
Half title page, 14, 40, 45, 47 *top*, 48,
72, 73, 85, 89, 96 *bottom*,, 105, 114,
118, 146

Cotswold Countryside Collection,
courtesy of Gloucester County
Record Office 91, 111

Cotswold Countryside Collection,
courtesy of Oxford County
Library 97

Edith Brill Collection, courtesy of
David Brill 74 *bottom*, 104, 124, 126
bottom, 143

Edmonds, Janet 76

Gloucestershire Countryside (June Lewis
Collection) 80, 98, , 149 *two
photographs*

Gloucestershire County Council 11

Grimes, S, courtesy of 154

Jelfs, David (June Lewis
collection) 94

Lewis, June Cover, Opposite title page,
Contents page *two photographs*, 15 *two
photographs*, 17 *top*, 18 *centre and bottom*, 22,
26, 27, 28, 37, 38, 39, 41 *four photographs*,
43 *two illustrations*, 49, 50 *three photographs*,
51, 53, 55 *two photographs*, 56, 58 *top*, 59,
60, 61, 63, 64 *left*, 65 *four photographs*, 67,
68, 69, 70, 71, 75, 76, 79, 81, 82, 83, 84
three illustrations, 88 *four photographs*, 93 *two
photographs*, 95, 99 *two photographs*, 101,
102 *top*, 108 *top and right*, 110, 112 *three
illustrations*, 113, 115 *two illustrations*, 116,
121, 122, 123, 126 *top*, 132, 133 *bottom two*,
134, 135 *bottom right*, 143 *right*, 144, 148,
151, 153, 155

Lister, Margaret 30, 145 *two photographs*,
146 *bottom left and top right*

Lovesey, Sarah 86 *left*

Nottinghamshire County Cricket Club,
courtesy of 102 *bottom*

Perry, David 108 *bottom left*

Peters, Ian 123

Playne, David 6, 13, 18 *top*, 19 *top*, 25, 49,
119, 130 *two photographs*, 136-141, *five
photographs and three illustrations*

Shipman, Juliet 23 *two photographs*, 34, 54,
58 *bottom*, 63, 86 *right*, 96 *top*, 157 *right*

Stokes, Colin 150 *two photographs*

Swanwick, Russell 133 *top*

Swinford, George 57
Vizor, Mary 66, 74 *top*, 107, 157

Wiltshire and Gloucestershire Standard
47 *bottom*

Yeoman, Ernest 52

While all possible care has been taken to
trace and acknowledge the source of
illustrations, if any errors have accidentally
occurred, the publishers will be happy to
correct these in future editions, provided
they receive sufficient notification.